LIFE *On* PURPOSE

by Gibson Sylvestre

LIFE *On* PURPOSE

Requests for information should be addressed to:
P.O. Box 934741
Margate, FL 33093

Website: Mylifeonpurpose.org

Printed in the United States of America.

Cover design by Aja Wilson

Layout design by Michele Scanlan

Photography provided by Liz Ordonez Photography

ISBN: 978-0-615-21166-4
Library of Congress Control Number: 2008905144

Presented To:

_____

From:

Dedication

I would like to thank Jesus Christ
for saving me and giving me the
strength and wisdom to write this book.

I would like to dedicate this book
to my beautiful bride, Brigitte.
You have helped me grow so close to our Savior.
Thanks for being a revolutionary for Christ!
I love you sweetheart!

Acknowledgments

With the utmost love, appreciation, and sincerity, I would like to thank all of you who have helped and inspired me throughout this colossal project. Words are insufficient to describe how grateful and thankful I am to:

My bride, Brigitte

Mom & Dad and the entire Sylvestre Family

The entire Gelin Family

All of our extended family

Barbara Lundy

Michele Scanlan

Allen Atsby

Pastor Bob Coy

Aja Wilson

Reggie Dabbs

Sammy Morris

Andrew Palau

Jeffrey Roschman

Wayne Huizenga Jr. & Family

Todd & Liz-Ordenez-Dawes

Our Calvary Chapel Fort Lauderdale Family

All the folks we work with throughout the globe to spread the Good News!

Table of Contents

Preface

Today, there's a cry and a plea of desperation for the fire of God. All the vices and man-made pacifiers just won't cut it anymore. God has His mighty hands on a people man considers "God-forsaken". Drugs, broken families, alcohol, religion, and worldly relationships have failed us miserably. Lies, perversion, and deception have tightened their grip on our culture. But in this critical and decisive time in history there is an answer. It's not anything man-made. It's not fancy tricks or man's cleverness. It's called the "fire of God!"

This fire burns with hope for the perishing, peace for the perplexed and divine power for the powerless! This world has yet to see what God can do with a group of people who are sold out for Christ. Can you imagine seeing millions and millions of believers, not just playing church, but radically seeking God? For them it's not merely about getting on fire for God at a conference or simply going through the motions – for them it's about living a life of total surrender to the King of Kings and the Lord of Lords!!!!

For they know their God and they are strong and will do great exploits for their God, for their eyes are on the prize! They don't care if they are ridiculed for being passionate about God. As Watchman Nee once said, "By the time the average Christian gets his temperature on normal, everybody thinks he has a FEVER!" They have a love and joy that is contagious to everyone they come in contact with.

We are a people that have been ignited by God himself. We're sick and tired of being sick and tired and we are unsatisfied with our satisfaction. As Jesus Christ said, *"I have come to bring fire on the earth and how I wish it was already kindled."* (Luke 12:49) Get ready! Get ready! Get ready! The fire of God isn't coming, it's already here.

We all need to wake up to God's purpose for our lives! We must rise to this momentous season with great expectancy from our heavenly Father. It's now time to believe and receive the fire of God!

Introduction

I have written this book because when I was growing up I almost died from a lack of hope, purpose, and direction. I grew up in a home that taught religion without having a personal relationship with God. I strayed away from my parent's religion because to me it was dead, fake, and irrelevant. I was forced to go to church and after a while I resented my parents and even resented the church. The enemy drove me into gangs and a life of crime where I saw a lot of mean things happen on the streets. I thought I was invincible. I rebelled against my parents and all other authority figures, but at the same time, I was lost, searching for some purpose, some hope, and a reason for living. There were countless times when I would wake up thinking, *What is life all about? Is there any reason for all this?* We go to school, get a job, get married, have kids, retire, and die. To me, the status-quo lifestyle didn't seem very appealing.

One evening I found myself recounting all the Bible stories I had learned when I was a child, and I began to turn towards Jesus. I remember a surreal peace that filled my heart in that moment and I began to weep. It was the first time I had cried in years, and the floodgates opened wide. It was there I met Jesus Christ - or should I say, He met me. This was my encounter with God. Have you had a life-altering encounter with God? If you haven't, then my prayer is that you would, because when you encounter God, you will be driven by a great sense of purpose and direction.

From that one encounter, I confessed my sins and my

sins were forgiven. Today, I'm a brand new person. I quit the gang and began a radical process of transformation. My parents and friends all said, "Just give him two weeks and he'll be back on the streets again." Nine years later, God is still at work in me.

Today, I'm in full-time ministry working with troubled and hurting young people. I travel all over the world to share the same love and hope I received when I allowed Jesus Christ to be my Lord and Savior.

The Lord has used many leaders in my life to give me this message of hope, love, and purpose. The message is simple: get connected to Christ and He will give you love, hope, forgiveness and an invigorating purpose for your life. I have written this book because I am absolutely convinced that God can use anyone to impact this world for Christ. I hope to see adults and young people uniting together to make a difference in this world. We all need each other. We need to learn to work together as a team.

Here's what I mean by team:

TOGETHER
EVERYONE
ACCESSES
MORE

We are not in competition with each other, but rather, we are in company with one another. In order for us to succeed, we need to stick together and work together. God is looking for an army of young people and adults to be a part of a great move of God. Let's not merely expect mighty things, let's attempt mighty things!

Growing in Your Purpose

For I know the plans I have for you, declares the LORD,
plans to prosper you and not to harm you,
plans to give you hope and a future.
- Jeremiah 29:11

The man without a purpose
is like a ship without a rudder...
- Thomas Carlyle

GROWING IN YOUR PURPOSE

I define purpose as a series of sovereign occurrences that catapult you into the person God created you to be. Our disabilities don't keep us from our God-given purpose, it's our doubts that do! When we doubt, we sabotage the plan of God in our lives. God has a plan for us. Our job is to add meaning to our lives by discovering God's plan for us.

WE ALL HAVE A PURPOSE

We all have a purpose. Knowingly or unknowingly we are heading towards a specified destination. Where are you going? Where do you want to end up? Indubitably, we experience unexplainable occurrences that seem to push us in a certain direction. From the womb to the tomb, God is pushing us towards a specified direction.

NEVER TOO LATE TO PURSUE YOUR PURPOSE

I once met a woman in the Dominican Republic who worked as a janitor, but her real desire was to paint. She was never given the opportunity to learn, but at the age of sixty-five, she picked up a paint brush and began painting. Many people told her she was too old to pursue her purpose, but she continued anyway. Her results were nothing shy of miraculous. George Eliot once said, "It is never too late to become what you might have been." Her paintings were exquisite and excellent, and today, they are a costly commodity in her village. For her, painting is her God-given purpose.

GOD KNOWS OUR PURPOSE

God is our Creator. He created us for a reason. Everyone has a purpose. How much money would you pay someone to tell you your purpose? Most of us wouldn't hesitate giving all we possess for that information. However, God has that information readily available to us. The way we find out our purpose is by seeking Him through the Bible. The Bible is our blueprint for life. God reveals our purpose to us in bite-sized pieces. In my opinion, He does this for two reasons. First of all, God does this because if He were to reveal our purpose to us all at one time, we would be too overwhelmed. In other words, if He were to reveal His complete Will, we would feel so overwhelmed that it would be more of a hazard to us than a blessing.

Secondly, God reveals His Will a little at a time to keep us coming back to Him. You see, knowing our purpose is all about relationship. God desires a relationship with us. Our entire existence is about our relationship with Christ!

YOUR FAMILY AND YOUR PURPOSE

No matter what our purpose is, it will involve our family. Our families can help us as we pursue our purpose. We are supposed to help our family members discover their purpose as well. We are supposed to mutually benefit each other. What are some ways you can help a family member discover their purpose?

If you don't have a strong family to lean on, God can provide other relationships to help you. Every successful person receives help along the way. Your help may come from your friends, your church, or other people in your community. No matter what your purpose is, it will always include people to help you, and as you are helped along the path, you are supposed to help others discover their purpose as well. God blesses us to be a blessing to others.

YOUR WORK AND YOUR PURPOSE

The majority of people either hate their jobs or lack a sense of fulfillment in their jobs. However, your current job is a part of your purpose. You may say, "I am a dishwasher at this dead-end job. How is this a part of my purpose?" Perhaps God is using your dead-end, dishwashing job to show you that you were made for something far greater. Perhaps He is using your job to build your character so that when He blesses you with your dream job, you'll appreciate it. You may say, "Why do I need to go to school?" God may have you there to learn from someone in your class. God has you in school for a specific reason. None of our experiences will ever be wasted. Cherish your current job position as a springboard to your greatness. Remember, King David had to learn to lead sheep before God trusted him with people.

YOUR PURPOSE WILL AFFECT YOUR COMMUNITY

As we search out our purpose, we must be a blessing to our communities in the process. There is a tendency to be so focused on what we are supposed to accomplish that we forget the needs in our own community. One time my wife and I were at Disney World and we were rushing to a particular ride. I was getting frustrated because it was taking longer than I had anticipated. My wife looked over at me and said, "Honey, you are so focused on the destination. How about enjoying the journey?" Most of us are too focused on getting to the finish line. Let us enjoy the journey along the way.

As you serve your community, you may actually discover your purpose. Never think of serving your community as a waste of your time. Serving can lead you one step closer to fulfilling your purpose!

YOUR PURPOSE IS IMPORTANT!

God made you for a valuable reason. Imagine with me that you got stranded on the North Pole, one of the coldest places on Earth. To make matters worse, you only had one match to start a fire that would keep you warm. What would you do? How careful would you be with this match? You would be extremely careful with how you used that match! Well, what about your purpose? How careful are you with discovering and cultivating your God-given purpose? Like that match, we only have one life. Let's not squander our time here on Earth. When we realize God is our sole purpose, it will give us our soul purpose!

DOES PURSUING OUR PURPOSE HAVE TO BE FRUSTRATING?

We can become off balance, but the fact of the matter is, pursuing our purpose doesn't have to be frustrating. We must maintain our balance as we go after our purpose; there should be a natural flow as we seek to fulfill our purpose. There is a sense of peace in our hearts when we are doing what we were made to do. God leads in peace not in turmoil. When it's God leading, you will always have a level head about you. If you are constantly fretting and worrying, then spend some time in prayer to see if this direction is really from God. Where God directs, God perfects.

WE NEED BIGGER DREAMS

If God is the initiator of your dreams, dream big! God wants us to have big dreams, but keep in mind that all of our dreams should exalt Christ in some way, shape or form. T.E. Lawrence one said, "All men dream, but not equally. Those who dream by night in the dusty recesses of their minds awake to find it was vanity. But the dreamers of the day are dangerous men that they may act on their dreams with open eyes to make it possible." What a powerful statement. Why do some dream big dreams while others dream for small things? Why do we limit ourselves so much? Will you follow the dreams God has for you?

GOD-SIZED DREAMS VERSUS MAN-SIZED DREAMS

There are two types of dreams: God-sized and man-sized. Man-sized dreams are small enough to be realized by human effort. Most dreams that come from God are inter-generational. In other words, God-sized dreams cannot be accomplished in one life time.

A God-sized dream causes us to magnify God above our limitations. When we are intimate with God, we tend to dream big dreams and plan great plans. Have you ever attempted something so huge that failure is guaranteed if God does not intervene? That is where you find the excitement. When you are consumed with the living God, dreams become dangerous. The only limitations we have are the ones we set in our minds. Human logic has limitations, but God's power is limitless. We reach our highest potential when we are closest to God – that's when we start to dream the impossible. I believe that God's favorite word is "impossible." When we say something is impossible, we give God an opportunity to show Himself strong on our behalf.

F.B. Myer put it this way, "We never test the resources of God until we attempt the impossible." So let's dream big dreams! We have nothing to lose except our fears!

MAINTAINING AN ENVIRONMENT THAT PROMOTES GROWTH

Our environments can make us either sink or swim. If we put ourselves in an environment that fosters spiritual growth, chances are we'll grow. If we surround ourselves with people who are lukewarm, chances are we'll be lukewarm as well.

Certain types of fish grow based upon their environment. For instance, if you put the fish in a fish bowl it will grow enough to fit in the fish bowl. However, if you take the same fish and put it in the ocean it will grow double the size.

If we make a conscious effort to constantly be learning and growing, God will position us to be godly leaders for the upcoming generation. We must purpose to grow spiritually, intellectually, and practically.

GROWING IN COURAGE!

I define courage as the ability to turn fear into fire. In life we must do the things we're most afraid of, then the demise of cowardice is inevitable! Courage is not the absence of fear, but the conquering of fear.

Some of the most courageous people you'll meet have fear. I once met a man who wrestles alligators for a living. I said to him, "Boy you must be as fearless as can be." He replied, "That's totally not true. I'm the most fearful person I know. I have just learned to conquer my fears and do my job!" We commonly have the same misconception. We think in order for us to achieve our goals we must be fearful. However, true courage controls fear and does not allow fear to control it. Do you allow fear to hold you back for the calling God has on your life? You don't have to live like that anymore. Find a spiritual mentor whom you view as a courageous person and ask them how they conquered their fears. Then cry out to God and ask Him to strengthen your faith.

FEAR PARALYZES FAITH ENERGIZES!

Whenever you set out to follow the will of God for your life, two things will arise: fear or faith. They are like two people living on the inside of you. One is known as the flesh and the other the spirit. Whichever one you feed is the one that will lead.

I've noticed that fear paralyzes us and faith energizes us. For example, I remember the fear I had when God called me to start a missions organization when I was in college. It was as clear as day that I was supposed to do it, but I was so afraid of failure. I thought to myself, *Where am I going to find the money to start this ministry up? How am going to find enough help?* I don't know enough! You see, I was focused on my shortcomings and fear instead of God's Will.

After one weekend of intense prayer and Bible study, God gave me enough faith to launch the ministry. I started to look at all God had instead of what I was lacking. I believe God saw my faith and moved on my behalf.

RECEIVE GOD'S COURAGE

God is the most courageous Being in the universe. When we ask, He gives out courage generously. While on our honeymoon, my wife and I went zip lining in San Jose, Costa Rica. By nature, I am really afraid of heights. I did not know we were going to be hundreds of feet in the air. I was afraid, but I didn't want my new bride to think I was a coward, so I simply prayed, conquered my fears, and zip lined from mountain to mountain. I believe God gave me the courage I needed to proceed. When we pray and ask God for His courage, God moves in awesome ways.

GROWING COURAGE IN YOUR FAMILY

One of the first places we should seek to give courage to is our family. So many times the people we love the most are fearful about pursuing their dreams. Home should be a safe haven and launch pad for our dreams. I remember when my younger brother started playing football. At first, he was afraid that he would get pulverized because he was small. But I encouraged him, and his first year playing he received the "Most Valuable Player" award.

GROWING COURAGE IN YOUR WORKPLACE OR SCHOOL

Times are changing faster than we can keep up with. Many go to work fearful. Some are fearful that they will be left behind due to technology. Others are constantly looking over their shoulders thinking someone will take their jobs from them. Working in fear brings out the worst in us. We even exhibit this fear in our schools. You may see someone excelling in a particular subject that you struggle with. Don't allow fear to breed envy. Instead, encourage that person and ask to perhaps study together. We must turn our fears into fire! When we turn our fears into fire, we are more productive and accomplish much more.

GROWING COURAGE IN YOUR COMMUNITY

Every community needs courage to survive. Every neighborhood needs someone to be an advocate for courage. Why not be that person? In many of our big cities crime, apathy, and corruption abound. However, you can stand up and make a difference. Have the courage to stand up for what's right. Go ahead and be the face of courage for your neighborhood. You may not be able to impact every neighborhood, but you can certainly impact your own!

RUNNING TOWARDS YOUR GIANTS

We all have giants in our lives. Giants are things that cause us to tremble with fear. I found that the best way to conquer fear is to confront it head on.

We see an example of this in the biblical account of David and Goliath. David had every right to be horrified by Goliath. Everyone was so intimidated by how humongous Goliath was that even the best soldiers in Israel wouldn't dare to fight him. David was the most unlikely person that anyone would pick to fight Goliath. He was too young and too small. David wasn't a part of the military and had no experience slaying giants. So why was David so bold? Why was he so courageous? Did he have a secret no one knew about? I believe David had a quiet, yet dynamic confidence in God. David was so close to His heavenly Father that he knew God would be with him. David also knew the secret. What secret? If you are going to fight a giant, you have to run towards the giant and charge him as fast as you can. Most people would slowly approach their giants. However, courage says run towards them, attack them, and fully rely on God.

BE COURAGEOUS OR BE A COWARD

We fall into one of two categories: We are either being courageous or we are being cowards. We can feel that we are the most courageous person in the world and still struggle with fear, but it is when we stop fighting and give into fear that we become cowards. What's interesting is that it takes the same amount of energy to be a coward as it takes to be courageous. What separates the two is a willingness to see things differently. If we want to see a mighty move of God in our daily lives, we must rid ourselves of fear. We can't conquer fear on our own, however – we desperately need the Holy Spirit. The victory will come when we are on our knees in prayer to the Father. The coward sees the obstacle and the courageous person sees the opportunity. Which one will you be?

GROWING IN TENACITY

I define tenacity as the ability to wholeheartedly stick to one's God-given goals without letting go. When serving God we should never let go! If something is worth holding onto, then hold on to it! When you are doing what's right and you are on the right path, never let go! If you are sure God has called you to something, never let go.

It seems that when we set out to do what's right, things always get difficult. In fact, when we are persecuted, the Bible says that's when we know we're making a difference in the spiritual realm. It is always too early to throw in the towel and quit. Failure is still wet cement. When we give up, the cement dries up.

HAVING TENACITY WITH GOD

We must have tenacity with God because God has tenacity with us! How tight is your grip towards God? What would it take for you to let Him go? I pray and hope that nothing would be able to separate you from Him. Love is the greatest glue that will keep you connected to God.

GROWING IN TENACITY WITH YOUR FAMILY

Many times when things get tough, the first thing people let go of is their families. Our families should be where we run to in times of turmoil. If we don't have a strong relationship with our family, we should find groups in our church that can support us. If you come from a negative family, find a positive spiritual mentor and nurture that relationship. Afterwards, use what you've learned to encourage and pray for your family. Being tenacious means fighting for your family. It also means holding on to hope and expecting change. Pray for your family and never give up on them.

TENACITY IN YOUR WORK

When you begin a task you should decide from the beginning that you will stick to the task until it is complete. God will be honored when we are tenacious in our school and our work. It is not how we start a project, but how well we finish it. Be like a pit bull. When a pit bull latches its teeth onto an object, it is nearly impossible to remove that object from its teeth. All things being equal, the tenacious person always wins!

BEING TENACIOUS ABOUT YOUR COMMUNITY

Be tenacious about your community! Is there a cause that has gripped you heart? Is there a social ill threatening your community? It is easier to give up, isn't it? However, we must stand for what's socially and morally righteous. God is looking for someone who will stand in the gap for our nation. Will you be the one?

I met a woman in Nicaragua who was tenacious about spreading the gospel. One time she was putting on a huge festival to share the gospel and invited me to be the main speaker. When I arrived in Nicaragua, I realized all that this woman had to do to pull off this large-scale event. Many had asked her to quit, but she refused because she had heard from the Lord. On the day of the outreach, we saw close to 1,100 young people come to Christ! To God be the glory! We cannot and will not give up; we must be tenacious!

THE TENACIOUS FIGHTER ALWAYS WINS

A boxer may be in the best physical shape and still lose a boxing match. However, if his opponent has more heart and knows how to take a hit, he will lose. A tenacious fighter says, "Yes, I have been knocked to the ground four times, but I will still rise again and continue fighting." This world needs more tenacious fighters. If our cause is wholesome and moral we should never back down. If our goals and purposes will enrich us while enriching others, we should never let go...never let go! Just remember, God doesn't count how many times we fall, but how many times we get back up!

ALL THINGS ARE POSSIBLE THROUGH CHRIST!

I define feasibility as the ability to stare doubt in the eyes and say, "Doubt, you're defeated!'" Do you doubt doubt and trust in faith? That is the only way you'll overcome your obstacles. In God's vocabulary "impossible" is nonexistent.

I had an elementary teacher who told me that I would never graduate from high school, much less be successful. She believed that I was despondent and would never amount to anything. There was a time where I believed her and allowed her words to be very crippling to me. But as I matured, I ironically used her words as a source of inspiration. There is something that happens in the human heart when we are told we can't do something. Suddenly we rise to the occasion. I recently wrote my former teacher a letter. Here's how the letter read:

> *Dear Miss* _____,
> *Congratulations for being one of the greatest inspirations in my life! Because of your unkind words, I have graduated high school.*
> *Furthermore, I have graduated from college. Thanks so much for not believing in me, because that taught me that no matter who doubts me, God still believes in me"*
>
> *Sincerely,*
> *Gibson Sylvestre*

WITH GOD IMPOSSIBLE DOESN'T EXIST

In God's dictionary the word, "impossible" doesn't exist. Is anything to difficult for God? Has God ever gotten perplexed by a question? Does God need our help? The answer is no! God is independently sufficient within His own self. When we connect with God He releases some of

His power to us. When we are humble and self-effacing, God can use us mightily! When we are self-righteous and arrogant, God is very limited as to what He can do with us.

ALL THINGS ARE POSSIBLE IN OUR FAMILIES

It is so easy to give up on the idea that our family situations can improve. Whether you come from a decent family or a challenging family, no family is perfect. We can all use some improvement. Faith unlocks the door of change in your family. If you believe your family life will never improve, then it will never improve. God can work a miracle in your family situation. We must remain positive and look for the good instead of the negative. We must learn to look at our families through the eyes of possibilities instead looking of only looking at the problems. See the possibilities in every difficulty instead of seeing the difficulties in the possibilities. If your son or daughter is strong-willed and hard to control, say "God is going you use that trait in the business world someday." Harness that trait but praise it at the same time. If your spouse is extremely frugal to the point that it annoys you, say, "Wow, God knew I would need a mate like this to balance the way I spend money." There is always hope for our families.

IT IS POSSIBLE TO ACCOMPLISH ALL YOUR WORK

The first step of accomplishing a difficult task is believing it can be done. When we doubt ourselves and our abilities, we sabotage our ability to produce at our highest levels. God moves when He sees faith. When we find ourselves lacking in faith we can ask God and He will freely give it to us. Many people work in hostile environments. We shouldn't approach our work like the little train who said, "I think I can, I think can, I think I can." Instead we should approach it with the motto, "Through Christ, I know I can, I know I can, I know can!" The Apostle Paul put it this way, *"I can do all things through Christ which strengthens me."* (Philippians 4:3) By God's Spirit we can move mountains!

IT IS POSSIBLE TO SEE A
CHANGE IN YOUR COMMUNITY

Drugs, prostitution, crime, and corruption permeate our major cities. When we look at the problem as a whole, everything seems so big and so impossible. It is not possible to eat an elephant in one bite, but it is feasible to eat an elephant one bite at a time. When we look at the ills of our communities, we should first believe that God can change anything.

The story is told of a young woman who was raped in broad daylight on a busy New York street. Dozens of people were walking around who saw this travesty, yet no one called the police. What a heartbreak! When the police asked a man who was a witness why he didn't immediately call law enforcement, he said, "I was in a rush. Besides, I figured someone else was going to call the police. That street is so crime-ridden that is was impossible for anyone to help." How sad. Many people believe that it is impossible to make a positive difference in their communities, so they don't even try. I believe that it is better to try and fail, than to fail to try. Go ahead - go out and believe God for change in your community, and then do something about it!

CAN IT BE DONE?

It is possible to do anything you want as long as you firmly hold that it can be done. My philosophy is that if something is worth doing, don't let anyone or anything hold you back. If it will contribute to the greater good of society, be relentless; let nothing come in your way! God will be the wind at your back. If you are involved in something that will bring God glory, don't give up!

GROWING IN EXCELLENCE

I define excellence as the ability to do normal and natural things with supernatural fervor and quality. Excellence is the art of performing a service or creating a product for someone else as though you were doing it for yourself.

If you were an aircraft engineer you would be faced with the responsibility of designing a safe and efficient aircraft. If the aircraft is faulty, the responsibility falls on him. However, if the engineer was actually building the aircraft for himself to fly his family around, the quality of excellence would rise to a higher level. Why is this? Because the aircraft engineer knows his children and wife will be on board, so he has a personal interest to make the aircraft safe and excellent. This is a good system of thought. Do things as if you were doing them for yourself.

A GOD OF EXCELLENCE

God is the epitome of excellence. Every sunset is an expression of His handiwork. Every human being is an expression of God's excellence. Excellence speaks of God's love for us. God definitely pays attention to details. He is ordering our lives in His excellent way. Do you strive to give God your best? He gives us His best in everything. We can never be perfect, but it never hurts to try. We should do our best and let God do the rest!

EXCELLENCE IN OUR WORK

The great painter Michelangelo once said, "If people knew how hard I have worked to gain mastery, perhaps it would not seem so full of wonder." God wants us to work hard so that He gets glory in what we do. Our work is a reflection of who we are. We should approach our work like an artist approaches his art. When we honor God in our work, God unlocks His blessings on us. When we do what we do with excellence, God opens the door for us to share our faith.

GROWING IN COMMON SENSE

Many people believe that Christians should not operate with common sense. However, the Bible is very practical. Now, there are times God chooses to move outside the realm of the natural; He is not limited to our finite ways of doing things. But common sense is still an important trait to be grasped. Robert Green Ingersoll once said, "It is a thousand times better to have common sense without education than to have education without common sense."

In short, we all need common sense. Even Jesus said, "Be as shrewd as snakes and as innocent as doves" (Matthew 10:16). We should use our common sense to help those who are struggling around us.

GROWING IN INTEGRITY

Integrity is doing what is the right thing, even if nobody is watching you. The fact of the matter is that there is always someone watching us, because God is always watching us. There is a French proverb that says, "There is no pillow as soft as a clear conscience."

Integrity is really the deep inner core of who we really are. Thomas Babington Macaulay declared, "The measure of a man's real character is what he would do if he knew he never would be found out." What sin would you try to get away with if you knew no one would find out? I pray we all ask God to change our heart to reflect His heart. We should strive to be the person on the inside that we portray on the outside.

INTEGRITY COSTS MORE

Several years ago I went to a fast-food burger place to buy a burger. That particular day I forgot my wallet. I was all the way across town and couldn't go home, but I had ordered my food and was in the checkout line. The cashier let me go and said it was ok to pay her later. I thanked her for her kindness. That night I remembered I had to pay her, but I determined that it was too inconvenient to drive all the way across town to pay her the money. Later that night God began to convict me. So I got out of bed, got dressed, drove for several miles and paid the woman. She thanked me profusely. I learned that it is always harder to do what's right.

WHAT KIND OF MAN WAS NATHANEL?

The Apostle John writes an account about a man who had impeccable character. His name was Nathanel. Concerning him, Jesus said, *"Now here is a genuine son of Israel—a man of complete integrity. 'How do you know about me?' Nathanael asked"* (John 1:47-48 NLT). What kind of man was he that God spoke so highly of him? How was his home life? How was he in school and work? How did he handle sexual temptations? How was his integrity when it came to business? I guess only God really knows the answers to these questions. But whatever he did, he sure was a man of integrity to have Jesus say that about him.

GROWING IN OPTIMISM

How do you view challenges in life? We should view problems as challenges. We must see the rose and not the thorns. We must be able to see the prodigal son coming home and hope coming from despair. The pessimist sees the problem in every opportunity, but an optimistic person sees opportunity in every problem. Concerning this issue, King Solomon writes, *"For as he thinketh in his heart, so is he"* (Proverbs 23:7 KJV). God wants us to be optimistic. Even through the painful parts of life, we can find hope.

OVERCOMING LOW EXPECTATIONS

We are living in an era of low expectations. Many people confine themselves to small thinking. In order to grow, we must be challenged. In order to be challenged, we must get rid of our low expectations. Do you expect big things from God or only small things? Today, ask God to give you a bigger vision than you could ever fathom.

Taking Action!

1. List the top two most courageous people in your life.
2. Write down their top two qualities.
3. What steps can you take to become more courageous?"
4. Write the name of someone who can keep you accountable as you set out to be more courageous. (Set up bimonthly meetings with this accountability partner)
5. What job would you pay to do?
6. What would you do if you knew you couldn't fail?

Read Jeremiah 29: 11-13
For I know the plans I have for you, declares the LORD, plans to prosper you and not to harm you, plans to give you hope and a future. Then you will call upon me and come and pray to me, and I will listen to you. You will seek me and find me when you seek me with all your heart.

Repentance Reaps Results

*The problem with some people is that
they'd rather pray for forgiveness
than fight temptation.*
- Unknown Author

*God doesn't count how many times we fall
but how many times we get back up.*

RENEWING OUR MINDS

God's love for His people is so great! Jesus died for us all when we were in the midst of our sins. When we were at our worst, He still demonstrated His great love towards us. But now that we are with Him, we are made brand new. God's Word calls us to renew our minds. We must change our world thinking to godly thinking. Before we ask for God's fire, He commands us first to ask for repentance. Isaiah expressed this heart best when he repented before God. *"I am a man of unclean lips, touch my mouth with your burning coals."* (Isaiah 6:5) Here, fire symbolizes holiness. Holiness is necessary in order to walk with God. In order to walk in our purpose we must first come to a place of repentance.

Notice how I didn't say perfection. We can never attain perfection. We can only put forth our best effort. Ultimately, we must rely on the Holy Spirit to lead and guide us.

God wants miracles to happen among His people. His plan is to show himself strong on behalf of His people. Can you imagine the dead being raised, the lame walking, the blind seeing, and people being set free from addictions from our mere shadows and more? In the Book of Acts, many sick people were healed by the Apostle Peter's shadow. Why isn't this happening now? The reason miracles aren't happening is that many of us don't want to consecrate ourselves for the purposes of God. Most of us try to fit God into our puny little boxes, but He simply doesn't fit.

GOD HAS MORE IN STORE

I once heard a story of a wealthy businessman who was stranded on the side of the road because his car had broken down. He tried to flag several cars down, but no one came to help him.

He soon realized he had to walk to the nearest gas station to call for some help. It took him over one hour and a half to find help. By that time he was exhausted and annoyed. He walked into the gas station, asked someone to use their phone, called his family, but no one answered.

Frustrated, he left and began walking towards his car. Suddenly he noticed a homeless man crawling out of the bush. Out of desperation, he asked the man if he knew where he could get some help. The man asked him what his problem was, to which the man replied, "My tire blew out and I have no tools to fix it." The homeless man assured him that he could help. He not only found some tools, but changed the tire for the man as well.

The businessman enthusiastically thanked the homeless man and asked if there was anyway he could repay him. The homeless man quickly replied, "No! I wanted to help out of the goodness of my heart." The businessman insisted on giving him something, and reluctantly, the homeless man agreed. "Ok, if you insist, just give me twenty cents so that I can catch the bus to the feeding hall." The businessman smiled and said, "Is that all you want? You sure you don't want something bigger?" The man replied, "No." The businessman then drove the homeless man to his car dealership gave him a brand new vehicle! They became good friends and the businessman subsequently was instrumental in helping him get off the streets.

The fact is, we frequently ask God for small things. We do this because our view of God is very small. We need to magnify God in our thoughts. When we have a big view of God, our faith also increases. Let's continue to believe God for the impossible!!!

REPENTANCE IS KEY!

The main thing we need to do is repent! Daniel repented for the sins of an entire nation. In his prayer, Daniel said, *"I prayed to the LORD my God and confessed: "O Lord, the great and awesome God, who keeps his covenant of love with all who love him and obey his commands, we have sinned and done wrong. We have been wicked and have rebelled; we have turned away from your commands and laws. We have not listened to your servants the prophets, who spoke in your name to our kings, our princes and our fathers, and to all the people of the land"* (Daniel 9:4-6). Daniel repented on behalf of his people. We need to cry, moan, weep and wait for the fire of God to consume our land.

Why would one man repent for the sins of thousands? The reason is that individual sin affects society as a whole. The fact is, there is a lot of sin within the church that needs to be confessed. Not only do we need to confess our sins, we need to acknowledge the sins of our nation.

Some sins are outward sins, and some are inward sins. God knows every single one of them. We need to humble ourselves and acknowledge our short comings. When we humble ourselves God lifts us up!

We also need to enjoy the Word of God. It is not a burden to obey God, it is a blessing! How often do you admit you're wrong? We must stop giving excuses for our sins; we just need to say we're sorry.

The Bible promises that God will forgive us when we turn from our wrong doing. Notice how I say "our wrong doing." I include myself. Yes, the preacher is included! Many times we give the impression that we are holier than everyone else. This attitude only brings division and separation. We need to admit our faults, turn from them, and walk in humility.

TAKING OWNERSHIP OF OUR SIN

How many excuses do you have for your sins? Do you think I'm speaking to someone else right now? Are you offended by me right now? Our flesh wants us to be in denial of our sins. You are trapped by your sins.

Here is the process of being connected back to God. First, we have to admit we have done something wrong. Before God shows Himself strong, we to admit we are wrong. Next, we must immediately make a bold choice to stop doing wrong. The word "immediate" means right away. Most of the time if we don't stop right away, we continue in our sin. Today is always the best day to get right with God.

Third, we need to ask God for forgiveness. Once I heard a man say, "God already knows everything so why do I have to apologize?" The essential truth is that we need to confess our sins as a daily routine in our walk with God. Confession shows that we are humble and ready to change.

Fourth and finally, we need to forgive ourselves. This step is critically important. Many times the enemy of our faith holds us down with condemnation. Romans 8: I says, "Therefore, there is now no condemnation for those who are in Christ Jesus..." If God doesn't condemn us, we shouldn't either!

LIVING RIGHT IS POSSIBLE

It is possible to live a victorious life in Christ. When we repent He'll set us free. Some say holiness will never be lived out in our land. Some say we sex too much, drink too much, drug too much, rebel too much and kill too much. But from God's point of view, things look different.

Whatever God calls us to do, He also equips us to live out. In other words, if God calls us to purity, which He does, He will give us the power to live pure and godly lives. God will always equip us to say "no" to ungodliness.

IT WILL GET BETTER

Repentance always proceeds His presence. No matter how dark our sins, God can always cleanse us. In Galatians, the Apostle Paul says, "Where sin abounds grace abounds all the more." (Galatians 3:20) In other words, the uglier the sin gets and the darker the darkness, the brighter the light.

When we look at the skies, the stars shine the brightest when the night is the darkest. The darker it gets in our lives, we must remember how much more glorious the light will be.

God's consuming fire will purify our souls. Jesus is coming to bring a proverbial purifying fire on His people. Are you ready to let it cleanse you?

It will purify our lusts, our pride, our selfishness, and our shame. We are God's symbolic cup. Currently, our cups are filled with dirty mildew and infection. He is cleansing our cups through our acts of obedience.

Furthermore, the Lord is going to put His Spirit in that cup and all who partake in this fire should be ready for a mighty move of God! Let's genuinely turn and burn for Christ's sake. Repentance means to turn from going the wrong way.

We must realize that until we've been recipients of God's grace, we won't be able to see His face. Grace always comes before His face, just as forgiveness comes before His fire! When we walk in holiness, we have a joy that is hard to describe with words.

Instead of making excuses for our sins, we should ask Almighty God to excuse us from these sins. When make excuses, we are only justifying ourselves and neglecting to change our ways. When we openly confess our sins, we allow the Holy Spirit to come in and clean our hearts.

STEPS TO GOD'S CLEANSING FIRE

We all have things in our lives that need to change. As believers, we can't walk around as though we are sinless. When we lie to ourselves, the enemy holds us in bondage. Let's look at some ways to invite God's cleansing fire into our lives:

REALIZATION

First of all, God wants us to recognize our wrong doings. The majority of the time we are unaware when we're doing wrong. We walk around with a sense of aloofness to our shortcomings. We purposely ignore the fact that we are straying from God.

This cavalier attitude hurts the heart of God. We must not merely recognize our sins but dislike them greatly. Do you have a hard time acknowledging when you're wrong? Do you have a deep hatred towards sin? God hates sin because Jesus had to go to the Cross for our sins. Every time we sin we should think of the Cross.

THE CROSS: He did this just for you!

Jesus paid a debt that He didn't owe. We owed a debt that we couldn't pay. Do you see the relationship? Do you see the advantage? Advantage for whom? Us or God? Obviously the advantage is for us!

Do you have a deep appreciation and admiration for what Jesus did on the Cross? We should all have not only these, but a deep passion for what Jesus did on the Cross. We can't repay Him for all He did for us. Jesus died in your place. When I think of the Cross, I'm reminded of how undone I really am without God. God punished His Son so that he wouldn't have to punish us.

Why did Jesus choose to suffer so much? It is because He loves you! The writer of Hebrews says, *"Let us fix our eyes on Jesus, the author and perfecter of our faith, who for the joy set before Him endured the cross, scorning its shame, and sat down at the right hand of the throne of God"* (Hebrews 12:2). What joy did Jesus really get out of suffering on the Cross? He got the joy of knowing you and I would come to Christ!

Today remember the Cross. The Cross speaks of forgiveness of sin. Remember the Resurrection. The Resurrection speaks of victory over sin. Also, remember God's love. The Cross speaks of God's infinite love poured out on us.

If ever you doubt God's love, think of the Cross.

DON'T BE IN DENIAL

Once, while I was in New Orleans on missions trip, I met a man who claimed he had never sinned. Naturally, at the very least, he was committing the sin of lying right then.

When I asked him if had ever stolen, he replied, "No, I've never stolen anything before. If I take something out of the grocery store without paying, God will understand that I don't have the money and I have to eat." Then I asked him if he had ever lied before, and he replied, "Well, no, I've never really lied before. If my wife asks me if she looks good in a dress, I will say `yes' even if it doesn't look good. The reason I tell her these half-truths is because I don't want to hurt her feelings." I thought to myself, *Man, this guy is self-deceived.*

Many of us view our sins in this nonchalant manner. We must remove the blind spots out of our lives and live a holy and clean life. We must also take time every day to ask the Lord to reveal any and every sin in our lives. Today, take two to three minutes to write down the sins you're currently struggling with. Then pray and ask God to reveal any more sins that you may not be aware of.

After the Lord reveals these things in our lives, He wants us to proactively begin to change them. One thing to note is that we can't change ourselves. Only when we yield to God's Spirit can we ever experience the transformation power of God.

Every once in a while I ask my wife Brigitte, "Honey, is there anything I'm doing that either hurts or annoys you?" The reason I ask my wife this question is because I love her and want to please her. This is how we should operate with God. We should want to acknowledge our sins to that we can please God.

REVELATION BY HIS WORD

The greatest way God will reveal our sins to us is by His holy Word, the Bible. The Word is like a mirror to our lives. The more we get into the Word, the more we begin to see how undone we truly are.

When this reality sets in, we should start implementing change. Concerning this matter, the prophet Jeremiah says, *"Is not My word like fire declares the Lord, and like a hammer that breaks a rock in pieces?"* (Jeremiah 23:29). Here we see in scripture an example of the Word being an instrument used to change our hearts.

A RESOLUTION OF CHANGE

Repentance demands change, it doesn't merely suggest it. Once we know our wrong doings, we must not wallow in our wilderness of worldliness, but gravitate to God's forgiveness.

God's correction should bring us close to Him. However, many of us allow our sins to keep us away from our heavenly Father. The Apostle Peter puts it this way, *"Anyone then, who knows the good he ought to do and does not do it, sins"* (James 4:17). I believe that Peter gives the most comprehensive definition of sin I've ever heard.

My mother used to say, "If you know better, then do better." We all know what's right and what's wrong. But we conscientiously choose to disobey God. When we make a resolution with God, we are saying we want to make things right.

Resolution is a very noticeable and measurable display. One of the best examples I know of is the story found in the nineteenth chapter of the Gospel of Luke about a crook named Zacheus. In the New Testament, Zacheus was one of the most notorious crooks – he was a thief in that he made a fortune by overcharging people on their taxes. The worst part of this ordeal was that he had the law to back him up.

But something happened to Zacheus when he encountered Jesus. He actually switched from being a taker to being a giver. He gave back to the people he had ripped off.

In short, when we seek to resolve a sin in our lives there will be some form of practical action.

Before I was a Christian, I stole a very expensive watch from a friend of mine. Years later, after I was already saved, I went to my friend and returned the stolen watch. It was so humiliating, but it was also so freeing.

Do you need to resolve anything in your past? If you don't do it immediately you probably won't do it at all. Most of the time, delayed action means no action. But in this case, the cost of inaction will always be greater then the cost of action.

REVOLUTION WILL COME AFTER REPENTANCE

In history, every major great awakening was preceded by a great move of repentance. Our God is not just a holy God. He's a holy, holy, holy, holy, God!

Fiery revival will only take place when habitual sin in our lives if properly dealt with. Suppose the Lord was sitting next to you, and you asked Him, "Lord, what would it take for our nation to experience a great awakening?" I believe His response would be, "My child, are you ready to repent?"

Please, please brothers and sisters in Christ, search your hearts and get right with God. It will make you, your family, your community, and our nation a much better place. God is too holy; He will never compromise His kingdom for anyone.

THE BEST WAY TO LIVE

When I was new in the faith, I used to watched several movies about the Lord's return. Most were about being prepared at all times for the return of Jesus Christ.

One question I always ask myself is, "What do I want to be doing when Jesus returns?" Personally, I want to be on a missions trip overseas somewhere. I certainly don't want to be doing something that doesn't glorify God. So the next time you're tempted to sin, ask yourself, "If Jesus Christ were to return right now, do I want Him to see me doing this deed?"

PROGRESSION NOT PERFECTION

God isn't looking for perfection, He is looking for progression. God knows He doesn't have perfect kids, but simply wants us to put our best feet forward. We do our best and God always does the rest!

Let us return to our heavenly Father wholeheartedly. When we repent we will see the windows of heaven open up to us. God will transform our land and His power will be unleashed. We must return to a heart of prayer. When we learn to seek God with everything we have, then we will experience the sweet fellowship of the Holy Spirit.

LORD, UNITE US AND REVIVE US

We are in need of a great awakening in our land. Repentance always precedes revival. I've heard stories about these amazing national and city-wide transformations that have swept through many cities around the globe. Bars go out of business because most people are at church. Crime rates drop significantly. Families are restored. Everywhere you go people are talking about God. This is what I long to see one day in this great land!

Take the next few days get together with some passionate followers of Jesus Christ and begin praying for a move of God. I dream of the day where all of God's children - Black, Latino, and White, Jew and Gentile - all join together to transform this great nation.

I long for the day when we can all simply love one another regardless of skin color, denomination, or culture. I long for a revolution of love - a love that is unconditional. When the secular society sees this amazing love, they will be tearing down the doors of the church to get it. They will not be able to resist the gravitational pull of Christ's amazing love!

Taking Action!

1. Take five minutes each day for the next 21 days and pray for a revival in our country.
2. Do you have a disagreement or issue with a friend or family member? Go and apologize and do your best to resolve the issue.

Triumph in the Midst of Tragedy

The ultimate measure of a man is not where he stands in moments of comfort and convenience, but where he stands at times of challenge and controversy.
- Martin Luther King Jr.

By perseverance the snail reached the Ark.
- Charles Spurgeon

TOUGH TIMES WILL COME
BUT WE HAVE THE VICTORY!

We're living in tumultuous times. Many people are concerned about terrorist attacks. Suicide is at an all time high. We are constantly being bombarded with thousands of violent images on the television screen. Society is getting more and more perverted in their expressions of sexuality. However, God's heart is still to redeem His people and fill us with His power. No matter how morally decrepit things get, there is still hope. Part of pursuing our purpose will include enduring hardships. In Christ, we will triumph in the midst of our trials!

The Lord has given us His torch to carry but the enemy is trying to sabotage God's plan. Thankfully, God is not going to stand by and watch the enemy take His children out. Our God is victorious, mighty to save, and always on time!

A SCHOOL SHOOTING THAT CHANGED ME

One example is the tragedy of Columbine High School. Two boys decided to open fire at their high school. Several students lost their lives. Two Christian young ladies named Cassie Bernall and Rachel Scott became martyrs for the cause of Christ.

This school shooting had a profound impact on my walk with God. When I saw how these teenage girls gave their lives to Christ, I thought to myself, If these girls can live sold out to God, then I can as well.

Most likely God won't ask us to physically die for Him,

but He certainly asks us to live for Him. Thank God, because He delights in taking dead things and making them alive. No matter what assault evil may try to launch on God's people, we will always win. In the end, the good guys always win!

ARE YOU SOLD OUT OR ARE YOU A SELLOUT?

When I first became a Christian, I was timid about my relationship with God. One time some of my old friends were teasing some Christians and wanted me to join in. I didn't join in. I had too much respect for God.

However, I couldn't sleep that night because I knew deep down in my heart I had sold Jesus out. I didn't stand up for what I knew was right. I prayed for God to supernaturally empower me with His power and boldness.

Although I can't express it with words, I have never sold Jesus out again. Instead, I became sold out completely for Christ! What was my logic? I thought to myself, All of my nonChristian friends are sold out for sex, drugs, and sinfulness. Why can't I be sold out for what's right!

Since that time, I have lost a lot of so-called "friends" - actually, about 99.9% of all my friends. At first, I was so lonely. Then God gave me an incredible burden to reach the outcast students in my school.

By God's grace, I was able to lead several of these troubled youth to Christ. They became my best friends. God gave me friends again. These friends were ten times more loyal and genuine than my previous group of friends.

WHY DO BAD THINGS HAPPEN TO GOOD PEOPLE?

Some people ask, "Why do bad things happen to good people?" This is probably one of the most perplexing questions of all time. For instance, Job was considered one of the most righteous men of his day. However, he lost his health, wealth, and family in a tragic way. Again we ask "Why do such terrible things happen to such wonderful people?" I don't claim to have answer for this challenging question. However, I know from reading scripture and personal experience, that God is sovereign in all things. In other words, God is aware of every single thing that happens to us. I take great comfort that God is sovereign. Many times in my own life God has given me so much purpose from the perplexities of my life.

A DIFFERENT EMPHASIS

Instead of putting the emphasis on "Why bad things happen to good people," we should emphasize "What good people do when bad things happen!" In Job's case, he worshipped. "The Bible says, *"At this, Job got up and tore his robe and shaved his head. Then he fell to the ground in worship"* (Job 1:20). It's easier said than done, but worshiping in the midst of our storms provides incredible comfort. It is in the middle of these storms of life that we typically ask, "Lord, why me?" I believe that asking, "Lord, show me" is a better question. Many times we must go through in order to get a breakthrough. Sometimes God uses our trials so that we can minister to others in the future. The Apostle Paul says, *"[God] who comforts us in* all our troubles so that we can comfort those in any trouble with the comfort we ourselves have received from God" (2 Corinthians 1:4). God uses our trials to be able to empathize with the sufferings of others.

QUITTING ISN'T AN OPTION

When we quit, quitting is made easier for another time things get difficult. We must rest in the fact that Christ will never leave us nor forsake us. Here is a poem I wrote about not giving up:

I'M NOT GIVING UP

In the face of adversity I will stand and not quit.
Through pestilent, treacherous terrors I will not quit.
Though a whole army rise up against me even then
will I stand. Though hard pressed, I'm not depressed.
Through despair, I will not fear.
Though struck down, I will not stay down.
Though I face defeat, I am not defeated.
Though all of life's possible problems hit me.
Even then will I trust in God forevermore.
In darkness, distress, and despair
when troubles won't disappear;
when life seems so unfair.
I will not give up!
Though everyone forsakes me,
I will not let sorrow overtake me,
But will allow God to break me,
So that only He can make me.

No matter what
I'll pray, persevere, praise, precede,
presume, prevail and press-on.
To see Christ's Kingdom come I must fight!
I'll keep my eyes on the prize
because there is no other option.
With my mind made up,
Heavenly treasures laid up,
The price of my life paid up,
Spirit stayed up,
No time to wait up
I declare I will never give up!
With no hesitations or reservations
I will not stop
And can't stop!
I don't give up! I can't give up and I won't give up!

TRIALS ARE NECESSARY

There are many promises in the Word of God. God promises us to give us an abundance of love, joy, peace, and much more. However, God also promises trials. The apostle Paul put it this way, *"In fact, everyone who want to live a godly life in Christ Jesus, will be persecuted"* (2 Timothy 3:12). How many Christians do you know who claim this particular promise of scripture? I presume not many. However, persecution is one of God's promises. Nevertheless, God never puts us through a test that He knows we can't handle. Allow me to show you a new perspective on trials. When you go through something

very difficult say, "God must think very highly of me."
Because if God is allowing you to go through your specific
trial He evidently believes that you can handle it. Here is a
poem that has me go through some difficult times:

*When God wants to drill a man and skill a man and
thrill a man when God wants to mold a man to play the
noblest part, and when he yearns with all his heart to
create so great and bold a man that all the world shall be
amazed, watch His method, watch His ways, how He
ruthlessly perfects whom He royally elects. How he
hammers him and hurts him and with might blows convert
him into trial shapes of clay which only God understands
and his tortured heart is crying and he lifts beseeching
hands, how he bends but never breaks whom his goodness
undertakes. How He uses whom he chooses and with
every purpose fuses him and by every act induces him to
try His splendor out. God knows what he's about.*
- Unknown source

God also uses our hurts to keep us humble. If we
break a bone in our body, when it heals, it becomes the
strongest bone in our entire body. God has to break us to
make our faith in Him stronger. Always remember when we
get to heaven we'll recognize the heroes by the scars they
have. For example, after a baseball game we expect to see
dirt and sweat on the uniforms of the baseball players. The
dirt and sweat serve as evidence that the player played in
the game.

ENDURANCE IS KEY

God always gives us the strength to endure. Martin Luther King, Jr. put it this way, "The ultimate measure of a man is not where he stands in moments of comfort and convenience, but where he stands at times of challenge." Trials actually reveal our true strength. Thank God, they don't last forever! Gregory Peck put it this way, "Tough times don't last, but tough people do." Trials test our will. The Apostle Paul said, *"Not only so, but we also rejoice in our sufferings, because we know that suffering produces perseverance; perseverance, character; and character, hope. And hope does not disappoint us, because God has poured out his love into our hearts by the Holy Spirit, whom he has given us"* (Romans 5: 3-5). God will never disappoint us. We should never give up on God at any time under any circumstances. There is always hope and God always has a plan!

UNSHAKABLE PASSION

The world is always trying to steal the passion we have for God. It seems like everything in this world is seeking to destroy our passion for Christ. Every day I am confronted with my own brokenness and the brokenness of those around me. We must resolve that our passion for God will not be shaken by anything or anyone.

Whenever we are engaged in a move of God, there will always be an opposition. My dad used to say, "People don't throw rocks at an empty mango tree. They always throw rocks at mango trees with fruit on them." In other words, the reason there is such an attack on us is because God evidently wants to do something amazing in our midst.

For example, imagine someone striking a match and accidentally starting a fire. Immediately, they try to put out the fire by stepping on it, pouring water on it, etc. Despite numerous attempts to put it out, the fire will ironically grow bigger and bigger. No matter how hard they try, the fire mysteriously keeps gaining more and more momentum! Can you imagine the fire in a move of God? God is for us and we will make a difference!

In the darkest of nights, the stars shine the brightest! God is with us and no one can stop us. God is taking us through the problem land so that we can get to the Promised Land.

In the Bible, the evil one asked to tempt Job. Why did he pick Job? In my humble opinion, he picked Job because he saw Job's potential in the spiritual realm. On the outside Job looked like an ordinary human being. But on the inside Job was a spiritual giant.

God has put greatness on the inside of all of us. The enemy of our faith is looking on at us and sees spiritual giants in the land. And he is so afraid of what God is doing in and through us.

On the other hand, God is going to and fro the whole earth, looking for some people. What kind of people is He looking for? The Bible teaches us that He is looking for some people through whom He can do some radical things.

He is the puppet master and we are the puppets. God wants to use each of us uniquely according our gifts and callings. He has a detailed blueprint for us to follow. Oh, I plead with you let His fire burn you figuratively. Let God empower you. He has promised that His resources will never run dry.

For our God is and was and is to come. Ask yourself, "How's my passion for God been lately?" Are you ready for God to use you? As God looks down from heaven will He find you faithful?

WHERE ARE YOU LOOKING?

Where we focus our eyes in the midst of our trials can determine whether or not we pass or fail the test. So where are your eyes to day? Are you focused on how big your problem is or how big your God is?

In the account of David and Goliath, David didn't focus on how big Goliath was, but rather on how big God was. On the other hand, the Israelites were focused on the size of the giant. When our focal point is in the correct place God will bless us. In the end, it was David who experienced God's miraculous power, not the fearful children of Israel.

If we look down, we're depressed; if we look to our sides, we are disappointed because humans always fails us. If we look up, we have the victory in Christ! The writer of Hebrews puts it this way, *"Let us fix our eyes on Jesus, the author and perfecter of our faith..."* (Hebrews 12:2). When our eyes are tuned into how big our God is, everything else seem so small. Even the giants in our lives look puny. Where are your eyes today? What are you seeing? Are you seeing the oppositions or the opportunities?

TURNING PROBLEMS INTO PULPITS

One time I was on my way to a very important meeting at my office. Before the meeting I had to pick up a friend from the airport. As I was rushing to drop my friend off, we got caught in some bad traffic. A huge truck carrying oil got turned upside down. The entire road was shut down. Needless to say, I was frustrated and upset. After standing still in my car for about one hour, I decided to step out of my car. No one could move. Many people we standing outside their vehicles. The people were getting extremely upset because the traffic stopped moving and all of us were late to our meetings. I decided to capitalize on the moment. I decided to start preaching since I had a captive audience. I began my sermon by saying, "Have you ever felt like your life wasn't going anywhere?" Many people started laughing; they appreciated the comic relief. I gave an altar call and several people came to Christ! That experience taught me how to turn my problem into a pulpit. God doesn't waste the trials of our lives. God wants to use our trial and tribulations to bring Him glory.

Taking Action!

1. Find a hurting person this week and sacrificially minister to them.
2. Are you carrying any burdens right now? Today, lay all your troubles at the foot of the Cross.

Rising Higher Than Your Current Location

A mind once stretched, can never return to its original condition.
- Oliver Wendell Holmes

Our walk with God is like an escalator – it's either going up or down.

HIGHER LEVELS

Things are constantly changing. We are either moving towards God or away from God. God wants us to go higher with Him. The problem is many of us are too comfortable where we're at. We must not be afraid to move closer to Christ. There is a great move of God from among the people of God. The bar is rising. The standard is rising. The empowerment of the Spirit is increasing.

God is restoring to us a new level of purity. God is birthing in us a new level of commitment. God never gives us more than we can handle. God will not allow us to remain stagnant. In order to pursue our God-given purpose, we must be willing to rise higher than our current location.

TIME TO INCREASE

There is truly no room to decrease the level of intensity, only increase. Our walk with God is like an escalator; it's either going up or down. We are never standing still in one place. Our faith is either increasing or decreasing.

Likewise, our passion for God is either increasing or decreasing. Morality needs to be maintained; purity needs to be promoted; and holiness needs to be desired. So many times we as the church like to remain at the same level and not be challenged to grow.

NO MORE TRAINING WHEELS

As small children it's permissible to have training wheels on our bike. However, it is a bit strange to see a grown man riding a bike with training wheels on them.

Spiritually speaking, many of us enjoy using spiritual training wheels. We want to continually stay in a state of complacency. God loves us too much to keep us is that state of mind. God is taking us up to higher heights and deeper depths.

OUT WITH THE OLD

The story is told of a mother and her son. The boy found an old teddy bear at a thrift store. The tag on the teddy bear revealed that it was at least fifteen years old. It was old, smelly, and unsanitary.

The boy's mother tried everything to get this teddy bear away from her son. But he had gotten used to it and refused to give it up. Night after night, as the child's mother tucked him into bed, she explained why she needed to take the teddy bear away. Yet the boy refused.

Then, in the most loving way, the mom revealed that she had gotten a brand new bear for the boy and in order for him to receive it, he had to give up the old bear. Once the boy saw the new bear, he immediately gave up the old teddy bear.

The Lord wants us all to let go of the old teddy bears of our lives. Why do we insist on holding on to our past? Why don't we trust God with everything?

THE MONA LISA

Leonardo Da Vinci's painting the Mona Lisa is one of the most famous pieces of art of all time. Today the Mona Lisa is worth millions of dollars. What would happen if someone were to change the frame of the Mona Lisa? Let's say they put the painting in a frame worth five dollars. Would the Mona Lisa be worth any less? Of course not! Our bodies are our proverbial frame and what's on the inside of us is worth far more than the Mona Lisa. The apostle Paul said, *"But we have this treasure in jars of clay to show that this all-surpassing power is from God and not from us"* (2 Corinthians 4:7). Paul was saying what lies inside of us is greater than what lies on the outside of us. Our bodies house the Holy Spirit. That is awesome! No matter what others may say we matter to God. God wants us to be secure in our identity in Him. He wants us to focus more on whose we are instead of who we are. We can rest in the security that we are precious in God's sight!

LEAVING THE COMFORT ZONE FOR THE FAITH ZONE

Choosing the things that make us feel comfortable is our natural inclination. If we had the choice of lifting fifty pounds versus one hundred and fifty pounds, we would pick fifty pounds. We either live in the faith zone or the comfort zone.

What is the comfort zone? The comfort zone is what comes easy to us. It's what's most familiar to us. For example, it is easy and convenient for me to hang with people who are into sports. I grew up playing sports and I can relate to sports on many levels.

If I go somewhere for the first time, I can easily converse with people about sports. In this case, sports is my comfort zone. Let's say I meet someone who is a science genius, I may not be inclined to talk to them. Why? Because talking to a science genius may be intimidating or uncomfortable.

What is the faith zone? The faith zone is an area where you are completely trusting God to lead and guide you. King Solomon declares, *"Trust in the LORD with all your heart and lean not on your own understanding; in all your ways acknowledge him, and he will make your paths straight."* (Proverbs 3:5-6) We step into the faith zone when we step out of the comfort zone.

The faith zone is very exciting. We see God do miracles in the faith zone; our faith stretches in the faith zone. We realize that God is all we need in the faith zone.

GREAT FAITH GREAT GOD

Several years ago, I witnessed God do some miraculous things while I was with a missions team in South Africa. We met a woman who had been paralyzed for over six years. While we ministered the love of Christ to her, she asked us to pray for God to heal her. At first we were hesitant. I had never seen anyone healed of paralysis before. But, we stepped out of our comfort zone and stepped into the faith zone. We prayed a simple prayer that God would heal the woman. Sure enough, God healed the woman!

God moves when we trust Him. People who step into the faith zone participate in the miraculous works of God. People who stay in the comfort zone are only spectators of what God does. Do you want to be in the faith zone or the comfort zone?

SOMETIMES COMFORT HURTS MORE

A young boy once saw a butterfly struggling to get out of its cocoon. So being a nice little boy he started to help the butterfly. He removed a razor from his pocket and began delicately cutting the cocoon. Eventually he managed to completely remove the beautiful butterfly from its struggle.

The boy felt good about the fact that he helped the butterfly. A few minutes later he noticed that the wings of the butterfly looked really weak and feeble. Then, after a few minutes, the butterfly died.

Somehow the boy felt that he had something to do with passing of the butterfly. So he spent that evening researching the different stages of butterflies.

He found out that butterflies need to break out of their cocoons by themselves. For the butterfly, the struggle it takes to break out of the cocoon is what makes their wings strong. If they get help breaking out of the cocoon their wings will never be strong enough to fly.

Likewise, we must go through struggles. They are necessary to our growth. When we take the easy way out we miss out on the opportunity of seeing God's power.

ENOUGH IS NOT ENOUGH

The move and calling of God isn't overwhelming or burdensome. Many times in life we've mastered the art of getting by. If we try to get by in our walk with God we'll do just that "get by." Do you want to simply get by?

Most Christians today live on the spiritual avenue

called "barely getting by". Why do we settle for less when God is offering His best? Jesus looks down on us and says, "Stop pushing My loving hands of holiness away." Right when our spiritual cups get past the halfway mark, we scream, "stop it!" We're afraid to let God in.

The fact of the matter is that the more of God we let in, the more our flesh disappears. In God's economy enough isn't enough. God so desperately wants to take us to the next level. Consequently, we're not willing. God is trying to get us to the serve Him with reckless abandonment.

We must become unsatisfied with our satisfaction. Why foolishly attempt to limit a limitless God? Are you satisfied with the crumbs of Christianity? How are you growing? What are you doing to challenge your faith? How is your purity, chastity, intimacy, integrity, loyalty and humility?

We've become so accustomed to the crumbs that the entire piece of bread becomes a task to be avoided. Callousness and insensitivity has its grave claws pierced in the very heart of some of our churches.

Some of us have stopped going forward for so long that we don't even realize we're going backwards. In God's economy there is no middle ground, we are either moving forward or moving backwards. We must sincerely become unsatisfied with our satisfaction and strive for more of God and less of us.

Jesus Said, *"From the days of John the Baptist until now, the kingdom of heaven has been forcefully advancing, and forceful men lay hold of it"* (Matthew 11:12). Here, Jesus is speaking of the His followers passionately advancing God's kingdom. God doesn't call us to be mundane. He calls us to a meaningful and adventurous life.

We must pray for a fire-filled passion that will catapult us out of our mediocrity and complacency. For God has called us to valiantly move forward. Are you discontent with your contentment? Are you satisfied with just the crumbs? Are you ready to say "enough is not enough?" When we get dissatisfied with our satisfaction major changes start taking place in our lives. Does Christ have all of you? What are you willing to surrender to walk in deeper intimacy with Christ?

A ROOFTOP EXPERIENCE

I remember a time where I was drifting away from God. I was so busy that I didn't make any time for God. I started see my passion for God begin to go lower and lower. Then one day I stopped in my tracks and called out to God. I grabbed a ladder and went on my roof. I went on my roof so that no one could distract me. I stayed there for hours crying out to God. Then God's presence filled my empty heart. I sensed the presence of God again. I was restored.

I firmly believe God restored me because I was desperate. I didn't care about anything else except getting close to God. Are you desperate for God? Are you willing to seek Him? Our desperation precedes His visitation. If you want Christ to show up in your life in a major way get desperate.

God is raising the bar on us because He wants to take

us further. What it took yesterday won't be sufficient today. God wants us to fully rely on Him. So do we find it difficult to rely on His might and power? We want things our way. We think we know more than God. We must repent for such attitudes.

We must let go of our puny portions and receive God's double portion. Once we let God control our lives, we will see His blessings multiply.

MULTIPLICATION VERSUS ADDITION

Man adds but God multiplies. In the gospels we read the account of a young boy who had a few pieces of bread and fish. He gave up the small amount of food he had and God multiplied. In the boy's hands, the lunch could only feed one person. In Jesus' hands, that small lunch multiplied to feed over five thousand people. What areas in your life you're still holding on to? Do you want God to bring multiplication in your life? If so, stop trying to add using your flesh. Put everything in God's hands and watch Him multiply!

GUILT MUST GO!

What will it take for us to rise higher? Is it attending more church services? Is it miracles? No, it's receiving God's forgiveness. Many of us have bought into one of Satan's greatest lies. The enemy of our faith tells us that God hasn't forgiven us. We walk around in guilt and condemnation.

Condemnation and guilt plagues the body of Christ.

We must realize that our God is a God of forgiveness. Guilt allows our past to paralyze us. Forgiveness allows God's love to invigorate us.

A GOD OF SECOND CHANCES
In our minds, we know that God is a forgiving God. But many of us haven't learned to walk daily in God's forgiveness. God is a God of second chances. He also is a God of a thousand chances. When we became followers of Christ; He forgave us for our past, present, and future sins. The Cross of Jesus Christ provides all the forgiveness and healing we will ever need. We are prevented from rising higher when we live in the past. Today, meditate on thoughts of God's forgiveness.

GOD IS NOT MAD AT US!
God is not mad at us. Psalm 103 says, "As far as the east is from the west so far has he forgiven us!" (Psalm 103:12) When we believe the lie that God is mad at us we are held back from growing stronger. The more we realize God's abundant forgiveness, the closer we'll get to God. When we walk in forgiveness, we will discover more and more of God. Rise up, oh you wounded ones! Don't believe the lies that guilt has told you. You are forgiven! You are accepted! You are His and nothing can separate you from God's great love!

Taking Action!

1. Find ten Bible passages that explain your identity in Christ.
2. Set a goal to memorize all ten verses.

Maximizing Your Influence
To Impact Your World

*All that is necessary for evil men to triumph
is for good men to do nothing.*
- Edmund Burke

*We cannot hold a torch to light another's path
without brightening our own.*
- Ben Sweetland

IMPACTING THOSE AROUND YOU

God calls His people to make a difference in the world around them. This world hears us talk about Jesus making a difference, however, they need to see it. Wherever Jesus went He made it better. Our goal should always be to make the people and places we travel better than before we arrived. A major part of fulfilling our purpose is helping others.

He gives us natural influence to affect the world with His love and His kindness. By God's power, we can have insight to be agents of positive change. When we see a problem, we should ask ourselves, "How can I make this situation better?" When we posses this mentality, God will give us the insight to make a difference.

WE'RE ALL LEADERS

No matter who you are, you're leading someone. In other words, you have influence over someone. Leadership can be defined as influence. God wants us to use our leadership to transform this world for Christ!

USING YOUR SPHERE OF INFLUENCE

We all have a set of people, places, and things that we have tremendous influence over. When I was in high school my friends and I would pray nearly every morning in front of the school's flag pole. We did it so much that we felt as though no one even noticed. One particular week extenuating circumstances prevented us from praying at the flag pole. Later that week, the school principal called me in her office. I was reluctant to go because going to the principal's office usually meant you were in some serious trouble. I walked into her office and we began talking. Then she said, "I wanted to know if everything is ok because I noticed you and your friends haven't been praying at the flag pole." I was shocked that she even noticed us. She then explained that watching us pray at the pole had personally impacted her and was making a positive difference on the school. In short, she asked me not to stop praying at the pole. The point is we never really know who we are impacting. No matter who you are, you are influencing someone right now. We must use the arenas we have influence in for the glory of God.

God never asked us to change the world, but He has asked us to change our world. What does this mean? God wants us to impact those around us. Are you an influential football player? Are you C.E.O. of a major corporation? Are you a high school student? Are you a housewife? Then God wants to use you. As long as you're living and breathing, God can use you.

WE CAN IMPACT THE WORLD

Through the power of God's Spirit you can make a difference! God didn't put us here on earth to simply serve ourselves. In fact, people who serve others have a greater sense of joy. We should constantly be asking ourselves the question, "What can I do to enrich the life of someone else?"

When we go out of our way to love and help others, God takes care of us. The story is told of a woman who decided to commit suicide. She actually jumped off a bridge into the deep waters. A businessman on his way to work saw the woman falling into the water and jumped in to save her. As he was still in the air he realized he couldn't swim. So he yelled for help. The woman who was attempting suicide saw him drowning, and decided to abandon her plan to save him. That day they both ended up in the same hospital room. It was there the businessman asked the woman, "How in the world did you fall of the bridge?" She replied, "This may sound funny but I was committing suicide. When I saw that you jumped in the water to save me I was blown away!!! I saw you drowning and decided to save you from drowning!" Saving the man from drowning gave the woman a sense of purpose for living again. When we help others we gain a sense of purpose.

BE AN INFLUENCE OR BE INFLUENCED

In the world today, influence is inevitable. Consider the story of Jesus' disciples. God used eleven men to spread the Gospel throughout the entire world. A motley crew of eleven turned this world upside down. Today, the gospel has been preached in nearly all the world. Furthermore, billions of people world-wide consider themselves followers of Jesus Christ.

LET'S INFLUENCE OUR YOUTH FOR CHRIST!

Many adults look at adolescence as a time of great uncertainty and turmoil. Some view them as being hopeless. However, if there is no hope for our youth, there is no hope for the future. Our kids are our future. When I speak at school assemblies, church youth groups, juvenile jail centers, and youth conferences, I make it a point to constantly be checking the pulse of youth culture. From what I've gathered from first hand knowledge our youth are crying out for hope and meaning. When I speak with youth I always say, "Having dreams aren't simply essential to life, they contain life within themselves." Simply put, youth need purpose. Without a purpose to live for, our youth die doing things that are foolish. We must use our influence and resources to impact young people.

GOD DOESN'T NEED ALOT

In the Book of James, James says, *"Consider what a great forest is set on fire by a small spark."* (James 3:5) God doesn't need many people to make a difference, sometimes He just uses one. God used one woman named Rosa Parks to start a fight against racism and segregation in the United States. If it wasn't for Rosa Parks, perhaps this country would still be segregated. God used one man, William Wilberforce to bring an end to the slave trade. Because Wilberforce acted, millions of Africans were spared the plight of slavery. God used one man, Martin Luther to bring about a reform in the church. If Martin Luther had not acted perhaps we would still be in the darkness without the Word of God.

IMPACT OR IMPRESS?

No matter who you are, God has divinely put you in the position to influence those around you. Mother Teresa put it this way, "A life not lived for others is not worth living."

When we impact others we have a sense of fulfillment and joy. We can impress people from afar, but we can only impact them from up close. What do I mean by up close? I mean we can only truly impact a soul by getting personal with our call. I heard a story of a teacher who made a profound impact in a challenging inner city school. The majority of her students had poor reading skills and were falling behind in school. But she made it her mission to make a difference in their lives. On the first day of school she challenged all of her students. She said, "Class, if I remember all of your names in the next few minutes you have to promise me that you will try your hardest for the entire school year." The class agreed to her challenge. Then she recited all of the names of every single student in her class. Her entire class was blown away. That year every single student in her class improved their grade drastically. A local newspaper interviewed a boy who had improved from being a failing student and asked him why he had changed so radically. He said, "The biggest reason why I changed was because I knew my teacher cared about me. It wasn't about the fact she remembered our names the first day, but she believed in us." When we genuinely care about people, God will open up a door to influence them for Christ! We need to have a heart for the people we minister to. People can always tell if we love them or not.

I LOVE MEXICO

Years ago on a missions trip to Mexico, God revealed some ugly things in my heart. My team and I were there to do some construction projects on a local church. However, God showed me that I didn't have a deep love for the people of Mexico. I was frustrated and was wondering why I felt a wall between the wonderful people of Mexico and myself, and so I prayed, "Lord, break my heart for the people of Mexico."

Immediately I began weeping uncontrollably. I must have wept for two hours straight. After that time in prayer everything changed. Everywhere I went God was opening doors and forming friendships. We were able to lead hundreds of people to Christ. I strongly believe that I experienced this breakthrough because the people sensed that I truly cared about them.

BE A LOVER OF ALL PEOPLE

When we love people, God does miracles! Jesus was a lover of people. It didn't matter their race, socio-economic background, gender, or culture. He loved everyone. If we want to be more like Jesus, we must be love to everyone.

A WIDOW'S REWARD

There once lived a pastor who led a powerful move of God. He was very zealous, genuine and sincere. He lived his whole life dedicated and committed to God's work. In his congregation was a poor elderly widow who led prayer meetings in his church. She went unnoticed and almost invisible. Years passed and both of them passed away to heaven. In heaven the pastor enjoyed a nice luxurious mansion arranged in beauty. The prayerful elderly woman also enjoyed a lavish mansion. Her mansion was one hundred times bigger than the pastor's mansion. One day, out of curiosity, the pastor went over to ask the woman about her mansion. He said, "No offense but I thought because I was your pastor I would enjoy a mansion bigger than yours - doesn't that seem right? She replied, "Son, think again. I've been praying for your salvation years before you were ever born." Though many people could see the physical impact the pastor was making, the elderly woman's impact was bigger in the spiritual realm. Many times we feel we need to be able to see the results of our work, however, the best results will be shown in eternity. My fellow soldiers be strong and remember God uses the simple things of this world to make the biggest impact.

GOD CAN USE ANYONE!

Many people believe that God can only use perfect people. However, God uses imperfect people to preach a perfect Gospel. You may say, "I'm not good enough and I don't have what it takes." Or you may say God can only use flawless people like the people in the Bible. The truth of the matter is, even the people in the Bible weren't perfect.

GOD USED MAD MOSES?

Moses couldn't speak very well; he had issues with stuttering. Moses even had trouble controlling his anger. Many times he let his anger get the best of him. Despite his shortcomings, God still used him to write portions of the Holy Scriptures. He also led over one million Israelites to the Promised Land. If God can use someone like Moses, don't you think He can use you?

A SHEPHERD BOY NAMED DAVID

David was vertically challenged. In other words, David was a short guy. When David rose to fame he was only a teenager. Most people would say he was too young to be used by God. But David had a deep passion for God. In fact, he wrote most of the Psalms in the Bible. In his lifetime, David made some terrible mistakes. David committed adultery and committed murder. However, David repented and was restored back to God. Some might have said, "David is disqualified. God is through with David." David suffered great consequences yet God restored him. Have you messed up really bad? Do you feel disqualified? If so, you're in good company. If you sincerely repent and draw near to God, He will restore you.

MORE UNUSUAL CHARACTERS OF THE BIBLE

Jacob struggled with lying and deceiving people and God used him. Abraham was an old man who struggled with patience. Yet Abraham was blessed and became the father of many nations. Peter was considered a coward. He was infamous for saying the wrong things at the wrong times. He even denied Christ three times. Yet God used Peter to lead a great revival in the book of Acts. In one day, Peter lead three thousand people to Christ. Noah had a struggled with drinking too much alcohol. Yet God still used him to build the Ark. Many times God uses us despite us, not because of us. As long as we are repentant, humble and in fellowship with Christ, God can use us mightily!

JESUS CHRIST'S IMPACT ON THE WORLD

All the words in the world couldn't fully describe the full impact Jesus Christ of Nazareth was had on this world. Jesus was born in a small town. He didn't come from a huge influential big city, and wasn't some famous politician who had all the connections; He wasn't some powerful business tycoon. He wasn't a multi-millionaire. He didn't have a PhD from an Ivy League school. Yet, He has influenced more people than anyone else in history. He has inspired thousands of hospitals that have cared for billions of sick people worldwide. He has inspired thousands of universities to be built so that billions of people would grow intellectually. He has been the subject of thousands of books and movies. He has inspired many scientific and social movements that have improved the quality of life for mankind as a whole. Many great rulers have tried to dominate this world by force and violence. But Christ has had supremacy over them all using love and peace. A natural by product of following Jesus Christ is that you will impact the world.

THE GOSPEL IS IMPACTING THE WORLD

The gospel is spreading all over the word. In Asia, approximately twenty thousand people receive Jesus as their personal Lord and Savior every single day. In China, approximately twenty-eight-thousand people receive Jesus as their personal Lord and savior every single day. God's Word is spreading like wild fire all over the world. How exciting!

Some studies show there are more people becoming born-again faster than the birth rate. Praise the Lord! God is at work. God is doing amazing things all over the world. We must stay informed and participate whenever we get a chance.

God is using these times to spread His gospel like never before. Via technology, the Word of God can get out to the entire world in a matter of seconds. How can God use your gifts to spread the gospel? We are simple, ordinary people who God can use to accomplish extraordinary things. God delights in using simple, ordinary people because He gets all the credit.

BE A LIGHT TO WORLD

In Matthew's Gospel Jesus says *"In the same way let your light shine before men, that they may see your good deeds and praise your father in heaven."* (Matthew 5:16) This world is very dark. When we walk with God, we carry His light wherever we go. Martin Luther King Jr. said "Life's urgent question: What are you doing for others?" What a simple yet profound question. "What are you doing for others?" Have you made a difference in someone's life today? Are you seeking opportunities to shine God's light? God calls us to be the light and salt of the world. Light gives direction and salt fights impurities and perseveres. Instead of retreating from the darkest of ungodliness we should run towards it with God's light. A Chinese proverb says, "It is better to light one candle than to curse the darkness." When light comes to an area, darkness must flee!

BE A SOUL WINNER!

Charles H. Spurgeon once said, "To be a soul winner is the happiest thing in the world. And with every soul you bring to Jesus Christ, you seem to get a new heaven here upon earth." Our lives can be used to win souls for Jesus Christ! When God redeemed us He left us here to be a witness for Him on Earth. God knows all the people you are going to impact in your lifetime. Why not ask Him to reveal those people to you? I can guarantee He will. He's done it in my life. So it's not about us, it's about others. Jesus is sending us out to bring others in. We must not be selfish with the blessings the Lord has given to us. Mother Teresa said "Let no one ever come to you without leaving better and happier. Be the living expression of God's kindness - kindness in your face, kindness in your eyes, and kindness in your smile." Don't allow your temperature only to go up to the level of those around you and stop. God calls us to be contagious. Impact those around you and grow stronger in Christ! Be a change and make a change for Christ.

LET'S GET BOLD FOR CHRIST!

When we walk with God, He makes us bold. The Bible says, *"The wicked man flees though no one pursues, but the righteous are as bold as a lion"* (Proverbs 28:l). Most of us remember the tragedy that hit our nation on

September llth, 2001. Some terrorists decided to fly two airplanes into the Twin Towers in New York City. Thousands of people lost their lives in that catastrophe. That same day I was at my high school watching what was happening on the news. Everyone in my school was panicking. Many students were getting signed out of school due to fear. One of my classmates was weeping because her uncle was in one of the towers and was missing. When lunch time came around, most students could not eat. They were very distressed. I felt so powerless. I asked myself, What could I do to help? Then I prayed. I said, "God, I'm a Christian. You've called me to make a difference. God please give me the comfort and boldness to comfort those around me." After the prayer I stood on one of the tables in the cafeteria and began comforting my fellow classmates. Although this was a public school, I used some Bible passages. I thought I was going to get in trouble but at that time it didn't matter to me. Before you knew it I was giving an invitation for students to make Jesus Christ Lord of their lives. That day over two-hundred students committed their lives to Jesus Christ! To God be the glory!

IF YOU HAD A CURE FOR AIDS. WOULD YOU SHARE IT?

What if you had a cure for AIDS? Would you share it with the world or would you keep it to yourself? There is a disease we are all infected with; it's called sin. The Bible teaches us that because of sin death entered the world. If we die without the cure, we spend eternity separated from God.

It's our job to speak the gospel, but it is God's job to save the sinner. At the end of the day, we can't get away from the fact that we have a part to play in the grand scheme of things. In Ephesians, the Apostle Paul says, *"For it is by grace you have been saved, through faith—and this not from yourselves, it is the gift of God."* (Ephesians 2:8)

God has given us the ultimate cure. Once we share it God does His supernatural work and lives are transformed for eternity!

LOVE COMPELS - SHARE CHRIST WITH MY MUSLIM NEIGHBOR!

I believe that Jesus Christ is the only way to God. My next door neighbor believes that Allah is God and Muhammad is his prophet. So one day we had a discussion on the gospel. Because of our strong friendship we could tackle this sensitive subject in a respectful matter. Why would I want to have such a controversial conversation with a Muslim? Because I love him. Love is the only motivation we should have when sharing the Good News with others. The Apostle Paul says, *"For Christ's love compels us!"* (2 Corinthians 5:14) Because our family showed this Muslim man Christ's love, he admitted to me that he believes that there is power in Jesus Christ! Find a lost friend and demonstrate the power of God's love!

ONE OF LIFE'S GREATEST DELIGHTS!

What's the most exciting thing you've experienced? For me it was witnessing my bride walk down the aisle. I remember the first glimpse I caught of her; she was glowing. I thought to myself, Wow, God is good! It wasn't difficult for me to be elated by my beautiful bride's appearance on our wedding day.

Can you relate to this level of exuberance and joy? We are called to the same degree of excitement about the Good News of Jesus Christ. In the New Testament, we see countless instances where followers of Jesus were thrilled to share their faith. Some even gladly laid their live down for the gospel. There is a sense of exhilaration and joy that comes from sharing our faith. That's why it's called the "Good News." Everyone likes to receive Good News. So let's share this message with love and passion to a world that is dying to hear words of life!

I CAN'T SHUT IT IN!

Sometimes we can get persecuted for sharing about our relationship with Jesus Christ. One time I was witnessing, and some people tried to harm me. I prayed and God delivered me unharmed.

Consequently, I became fearful about sharing my faith and decided to stop. Then I remembered the words of the prophet Jeremiah: *"But if I say I'll never mention the Lord or speak in his name, his word burns in my heart like a fire. It's like a fire in my bones. I am worn out trying to hold it in! I can't do it!"* (Jeremiah 10:9) Before I knew it, God restored my joy, restored my boldness and then He removed the fear that had paralyzed me. Leonard Ravenhill put it this way, "A man who is intimate with God will never be intimidated by men." Let's not let fear stop us, instead let's stop fear by the transforming love of Christ!

APOLOGIZING FOR THE CHURCH

Let's remove the barrier of hypocrisy. Mahatma Gandhi, the father of non-violent protest once said, "I would have become a Christian if I'd met one." Wow, how sad.

Many times when I evangelize, I typically start off with an apology for some the hypocrisy of the church. Granted, none of us are perfect, but we certainly have a responsibility to live godly lives. I once met a man who was hurt by Christians. I repented on behalf of them. He sensed my empathy and sincerity. We talked about the gospel and he prayed to receive Christ. Tears of forgiveness and cleansing fell from his eyes. God wants to restore broken lives to Himself. Find someone who has backslidden or has been burned by the church sincerely apologize; share God's love and watch God move!

LIVE IT BEFORE YOU SPEAK IT

It is so easy to preach the Word, but it is so much more difficult to live it. Most of the time, the reason the world isn't impacted by us is because we don't live what we preach. Our actions are speaking so loudly that the world can't even hear our words. Hypocrisy is one of the greatest threats to the church. Before I try to evangelize to a non-believer, I try to earn my right to speak to them first. How do we earn the right? First, by valuing every person you come in contact with. Secondly, simply serve them. When we serve others it is a sign of humility. When we are walking in integrity and humility, God will give us the opportunity to be a witness for Christ.

A few years ago, I was invited to speak at an evangelism conference. I was scheduled to address a group of people on sharing their faith with non-believing friends and family members. My problem was that I hadn't shared my faith with anyone in more than four weeks. Needless to say, I felt very hypocritical. Here I was addressing all these people on a subject I myself wasn't practicing. My conscious beat me up. Now I try to live what I preach as best as I can. I'm not perfect, but I do my best.

COUNTING THE COST

Being a Christian is impossible without God's supernatural strength. A man once asked me, "If I become a Christian, will all my problems magically disappear?" I replied, "If you become a Christian you may suddenly have more problems and hardships." We pray for God to take the burdens off our backs. Instead we should pray for God to make our backs stronger. In Luke, Jesus says, *"If anyone wants to follow Me, he must give up himself and his own desires. He must take up his cross everyday and follow Me."* (Luke 9:23) Every great accomplishment had a great cost connected to it.

Diana was a new Christian who was saved from drugs and partying. One day, her old friends asked her to go partying again. She replied, "I can't do that anymore, that was the old Diana!" When we share our faith we must also ask people to count the cost. We must let them know that it will be difficult. We all have trials and tribulations. We let them know that saying "yes" to Jesus Christ means saying "no" to all other gods. We must all count the cost of following Jesus.

A PERSONAL TESTIMONY DOES WONDERS!

No one can dispute the power of your personal testimony. A missions team and I were in San Jose, Costa Rica ministering to some college students. It was there that I met Juan. I must say, Juan was probably one of the smartest people I ever met. He spoke five languages and was well versed in world philosophy. He began intellectually attacking Christianity. I shared virtually all the scientific, archeological, and historic evidence I knew about Christ. Still Juan wanted to argue.

Then I shared my personal story of how I came to Christ. Juan listened in utter amazement. He didn't accept Christ but he admitted that he was interested in finding out more information about Him. Revelations 12:11 says, *"They overcame him by...the word of their testimony..."* When we share how God has rescued us, God's power is unleashed!

YOU'RE SOMEONE'S CHANCE TO GOD TODAY!

In 2 Corinthians 5 the Apostle Paul says that God has given us a mission to draw people to Jesus Christ. There's a difference between having to do something versus having the privilege to do something. In our case we get the joy of sharing hope to a lost and dying world. God wants to use you to make a difference in someone's life today! When you wake up in the morning, look yourself in the mirror and say, "I'm someone's chance to God today!" Today, find someone in a store or mall and simply say, "Jesus loves you." It will change their lives forever! God may even open the door for you to share the Good News with them. If so, you can tell them about God's forgiveness and lead them in a prayer to receive Christ. When you experience this joy you will never be the same!

STOP PRACTICING HERMIT CHRISTIANITY

Christians often have a repulsive attitude towards the world. In other words, we sometimes prefer to distance ourselves from society. Sometimes we do this because we are afraid to be contaminated by the filth and immorality of our culture. However, we must practice balance in this area. We need to be involved in all sectors of society to make an impact for Christ. If we retreat we will inevitably lose the fight. It is impossible for a football team to win a game if they fail to show up to the game. We must show up in our communities as a visible and tangible beacon of hope and life.

USING YOUR RESOURCES WISELY

Our talent is a primary avenue to impact our world. What comes natural to you? What is difficult to others yet is easy to you? Whatever the answer is, that's the area God can use to significantly impact others. If you are a great athlete, use your ability to impact your teammates for Christ. If you have a natural inclination for business, use that ability to glorify God.

TIME IS A TOOL

Time is another important component in impacting others for Christ. Time is a gift from God. Did you know that "time" is the most-used word in the English language. It is possible to regain money lost. But it is impossible to regain time lost. How are you utilizing your time to impact others? Are you making the most of your time? Do you have a sense of urgency in sharing the Good News? God wants us to strategically use our time to leave a mark on this world. How will you use your time to impact others for Christ?

Taking Action!

1. Make a list of five unsaved family members and friends.
2. Take at least one unsaved friend or family member out to lunch this week and simply share your testimony.
3. Continuously pray for their salvation.

Desperation That Leads To Saturation

*If I find in myself a desire which no experience
in this world can satisfy,
the most probable explanation is
that I was made for another world.*
- C.S. Lewis

*The degree of your desperation
will always determine
the degree of God's saturation.*

ARE YOU CONSUMED YET?

Have you ever been consumed with something before? I remember being consumed with excitement the night I asked my wife to marry me. I was on a natural high for weeks. Everyone around me noted how ecstatic I was. God wants to consume us. When we encounter God, we can't help but be overwhelmed by His glorious presence. Concerning this matter, the writer of Hebrews says, *"For our God is a consuming fire"* (Hebrews 12:29). The Holy Spirit is a gentleman. He will not force Himself on us. As we submit ourselves to the Spirit, He fills us with His presence. But if we close the door to the Spirit, He backs away. Are you desperate for a taste of the living God?

MORE OF GOD, LESS OF ME

No one throws paper into fire and expect to retrieve its remains. That would be absurd. My desire is to have more of God and less of me. When we come in contact with God's consuming fire we decrease and God increases. All of a sudden it becomes all about Christ. Instead of saying, "My will be done" we say "Thy will be done."

BE HUMBLE OR BE HUMBLED

We have a choice to either be humble or be humbled. God wants all of His children to be humble. It's not about us. Many times we think the world revolves around us. The world revolves around Christ, not us. As we follow Christ, He will see to that we walk in humility. If we don't walk in humility, God will allow circumstances in our lives to produce humility. God cannot fill a man if he is filled with himself. We must let go of our pride. When we empty ourselves of pride, Christ comes inside.

WHAT CONSUMES US CONTROLS US

When you wake up in the morning, what's the first thing you think of? Before you go to sleep at night, what's the last thing that comes to your mind? What is the subject of your daydreams? What keeps you up late at night? Whatever your responses are is what consumes you. For instance, there was a time when basketball consumed my life. I thought of basketball first thing in the morning and all throughout the day. I was consumed with basketball in an unhealthy way. Basketball controlled my life. I have found that whatever consumes us also controls us. When we desire something, we develop an insatiable craving for it. However, nothing on earth can satisfy us like Christ can.

GOD IS OUR MANUFACTURER

God is our manufacturer. Because He made us, He knows what we need to operate at our highest potential. He has given us a manual which is the Word of God. Throughout the Bible, God says that only He will be able to satisfy us. No object or person will be able to fulfill us like God can. When we stay connected to God our Manufacturer, we find true satisfaction. In the ant world, all the ants are controlled by one chief ant. As many as 30,000 ants can be governed by one single ant. When that one ant dies, that entire population of ants go into a frenzy. Many of the ants suffer due to a lack of leadership and direction. That is how man is without God. When we are connected to God, we operate at our best. When we are disconnected from God, our entire life is in shambles. Let's stay connected to our wonderful God!

THIRSTY FOR GOD?

King David had an insatiable desire for God. Concerning this he said, *"As the deer pants for streams of water, so my soul pants for you O God"* (Psalm 42:1). Personally, I have been that hungry for God. God is attracted to spiritual hunger. When we seek God with all our hearts, He fills us until our cups overflow. Do you have a strong desire for God? Do you want God to bring a personal revival in your heart? When was the last time you wept because you felt distant from God? I love writing love poems to the Lord. Here is a poem I wrote after a time of seeking God's face. Here's the poem:

My Heart Burns For You
I'm consumed with desire
And my heart passionately is set on fire.
Like a child yearns for the milk of his mother
So my soul thirsts for you.
My spirit desperately pursues you.
I'm addicted to you.
Affections for you burn deeply within.
Longing so fervently I run after you with all I've got.
My passion is brewing my heart is so hot!

DESPERATION PRECEDES SATURATION

When we become truly desperate for God, He moves mightily! In fact, desperation precedes saturation. I remember visiting a gypsy church in Romania. In most of Europe the gypsies are a despised people group. Most people associate them with trickery and immorality. When I visited that gypsy church, I experienced desperation like never before. The gypsies were desperate for God. During worship they were seeking God with everything they had. That day I sensed the presence of God in mighty way. God's presence had saturated that service. Are you desperately in love with the Savior? If not, get on your knees, pray, seek God's face and watch God move!

Taking Action!

1. How desperate are you for God's presence? (On a scale of 1 to 5; five is the highest)
2. Take one hour this week and spend some time singing, praying, and seeking God's face.

Maintaining Your Passion For God

I have but one passion - it is He, it is He alone.
- Count Zinzindorf

Do not put out the spirit's fire.
- 1 Thessalonians 5:19

DAILY REPENTANCE MAINTAINS PASSION

God's hand is not too short that He can't save us, but it's our sins that keep us from Him. Our own sinful desires alienate us from God. We must learn to confess our sins as God convicts us.

I like to call immediate repentance the "clean sink principle." Our heart is like the sink. Every time we sin, it is like a dirty dish placed in the sink. If we continue this process, we will have a sink filled with dirty dishes. To avoid a sink filled with dirty dishes, we must wash each dish as we dirty them. For example, every time we sin we should repent for it immediately. If we repented immediately after we sin we will find that our conscious will constantly be clean. Then, at the end of the day, we can rest in peace knowing that we are right with God. When we live clean lives, we remain passionate about God. I'm convinced that one of the quickest prayers God answers is "Lord show me if there is anything in my life that offends you, and please Lord forgive me." When we genuinely repent, God restores us.

RENEWING OUR FAITH

It is fascinating to note that the word "faith" is only used twice in the entire Old Testament. However, all throughout the Old Testament we see the word "faithfulness." Why is the word "faith" used so infrequently? Because the Hebrew language is so descriptive that faith can only be expressed as a form of action. An example would be Abraham trusting God so completely - even if it meant sacrificing his only son Isaac.

Faith is something that should be something seen in our actions. The best way to build faith is through reading God's Word. We will remain passionate about Christ as we continually exercise our faith. Concerning faith, the Apostle Paul said, *"Consequently, faith comes from hearing the message, and the message is heard through the word of Christ"* (Romans 10:17). God's recipe for building faith is scripture reading.

DEVOTIONAL TIME WITH GOD

In the Old Testament, God gave the children of Israel fresh manna from heaven morning by morning. I believe this is symbolic of how God wants us to be in the Word on a daily basis. How much daily time do you spend alone with God? How important is your devotional life? Would you go without eating for two months? Of course you wouldn't. You would starve. In the same way, when we neglect spending time with the Lord, we are starving ourselves spiritually. Most of us don't make spending time with God a priority. God longs for intimacy with us. Do you long to be intimately in love with God? If so, make it a habit to take spiritual retreats. This includes taking time off and going somewhere for the sole purpose of drawing closer to God. God wants to humble us in private so that He can exalt us in public. Jesus wants to pull you aside and refresh your soul. When we seek God, He will love us and show us great and mighty things. As air is critical to sustaining life in our physical bodies, so is God's Word in sustaining spiritual life in our souls.

BEING A PART OF THE BODY OF CHRIST

God never intended for us to walk the Christian life alone. Many people say, "I don't go to church because people in church are such hypocrites." However, not all churches are hypocritical. The real problem is people looking for a perfect church. But there is no such thing as a perfect church. If you were to find a perfect church and join it, it would not be a perfect church anymore. Why? Because you are not perfect. None of us is perfect. There's nothing wrong with taking some time to search for a church that suits your needs. Just make sure the church's doctrine lines up with the Bible. In the church we find community, accountability, and opportunities to serve our community.

PRAYER IS OXYGEN TO THE SOUL

Show me a Christian that is not praying, and I'll show you a Christian that is straying. Martin Luther once said, "Pray, and let God worry." We lay our burdens down at the foot of the Cross. Prayer helps us to grow in our walk with God. A Christian will never ever rise above his or her prayer life. Prayer is oxygen to the soul. Prayer is critical to our spiritual life.

PRAYER IS A PRIVILEGE

The highest place for any believer is down on his or her knees. Prayer is one of the greatest privileges God gives us. Most believers don't realize the privilege of prayer. In prayer, we have the privilege to approach the most powerful being in the universe.

LACK OF CONFIDENCE PRODUCES
A LACK OF PRAYER

Many people lack the confidence that God will answer their prayers. Their lack of confidence produces a lack of prayer. Lack of prayer produces a lack of results. Do see the vicious cycle? The only way to break this cycle is through prayer. The more we pray, the more we see God at work. The cure for prayerlessness is prayer itself.

PRAYER IS A SIGN OF HUMILITY

When we pray, we are humbling ourselves. Prayer is one of the highest forms of humility. Prayer reveals one's dependence on God's strength and not our own strength. When I pray, I realize that I am the great "I'm not" and God is the Great "I Am."

DON'T QUENCH THE FIRE

There are many things in this world fighting for our attention. It seems like we are being attacked on all sides. The world, religion, and Satan is fighting to quench the fire of God in us. It is for that reason the apostle Paul declared, *"Do not put out the spirit's fire"* (I Thessalonians 5:19). The world would like to snuff out our passion for God. Has the world been threatening your fire lately? Have you lost sight of your first love?

THE WORLD WANTS US TO STOP

The world hates the light because light dispels the darkness. Jesus said, *"Everyone who does evil hates the light, and will not come into the light for fear that his deals*

100 LIFE *On* PURPOSE

will be exposed" (John 3:20). One of the ways the world tries to fight against us is through intimidation. The world tries to manipulate believers to tune out God's voice. The world also tries to ridicule us and tries to get us to keep our mouths closed about God's truth. The enemy tries to get us to focus on earthly things instead of heavenly. In the Book of Matthew, Jesus says, *"the one who received the seed that fell among the thorns is the man who hears the word, but the worries of this life and the deceitfulness of wealth choke it, making it unfruitful."* (Matthew 13:22) The enemy wants us to be unfruitful. He knows he can't take away our salvation but seeks to eliminate our effectiveness. Have the worries of this life been weighing you down lately? If so, remember, this world is not our home. Heaven is our home. Let's regain our focus on eternal matters. In order for us to maintain our passion for Christ, we must not let the world stop us.

RELIGION WILL NOT WORK

There is a drastic difference between having religion and having a relationship with Christ Jesus. Religion says going to church makes you right with God. I often ask people, "Does going to Mc Donald's make you a Big Mac?" Of course it doesn't. In the same way, going to church doesn't make us Christians. We must all accept Jesus Christ as our Lord and Savior. Religion says do good in order to get God. A person in a relationship with Christ does what is right because they're right with God. Do you see the difference? Relationship brings salvation and gives inspiration, religion on the other hand results in perspiration. Legalism brings about religious work without relationship. The enemy's temptation is to get believers working so much that they get burnt out. God wants to empower every believer with supernatural strength so that they don't burn out. For instance, when Moses met God at the burning bushing why didn't the bush get consumed by the fire? The reason the bush didn't burn out was because it wasn't set on fire by man but by God. Once someone's heart is set on fire with the law he burns out. However, if someone's heart is set on fire with Gods love he burns forever!

BEWARE OF SUBTLE DISTRACTIONS

It is so easy to get distracted from God's purposes in our lives. Many times it's the small and subtle distractions that get the best of us. The Bible says, *"But my eyes are fixed on you, O Sovereign Lord; in you I take refuge do not give me over to death"* (Psalm 141:8). The fact is, when we take our eyes off of Jesus we allow distraction to take over our hearts. In Revelation two verse four Jesus says, "Yet I hold this against you: You have forsaken your first love. Remember the height from which you have fallen!" We don't go away from our first love overnight. This happens slowly over time. It happens when we allow small distractions to shift our focus. Remember what happened to Peter when he took his eyes off of Jesus? He started sinking in the water. Was there ever a time in your life when you were closer to Jesus than you are now? If so, you have fallen from where God wants you to be. All you have to do is come back to Him. He's not upset with you. He's waiting for you to come back home to Him. Remember, you could be one million steps away from Christ, but it only takes one step of love to get back.

Taking Action!

1. Write down the top three people, places, and things that distract you from God.
2. What course of action can you take to avoid the things that distract you from Christ?

A Passion That Turns Into Compassion

*I would rather feel compassion
than know the meaning of it.*
- Thomas Aquinas

*We can do no great things,
only small things with great love.*
- Mother Teresa

COMPASSION IS A WAY OF LIFE

The true evidence of someone's passion for God is their ability to show compassion to others. When we show others compassion, we are being the hands and feet of Jesus Christ. Love is the mark of every true Christian. Not too long ago I was at a gas station and a woman approached me asking for some gas money. Apparently she was experiencing some difficulty with her credit card. I agreed to put some gas in her car. As I was pumping the gas for the woman, she was on her phone. She never once looked towards me or said anything. After a few minutes, she rudely asked if I was finished and then drove off. I was blown away by the fact that she never said, "Thank-you." I have to admit I was terribly hurt. I felt God began to convict my heart. I heard Him say to me, "Gibson, you are supposed to be compassionate to people no matter what." That day I learned a valuable lesson about compassion. I learned that we are supposed to be compassionate. When a car drives, it doesn't impress anyone because cars are manufactured to drive. When a cook cooks, no big deal because cooks are supposed to cook. When a Christian shows compassion, it's no big deal. A Christian is made to do good things. Many times when we give to others we expect something in return. Instead of giving to give, we typically give to get. God wants us to give to others and leave the results up to Him.

ACTS OF COMPASSION ARE A BOLD STATEMENT

The greatest need in the world today is not knowledge but compassion. Some of the smartest people of all time have been the most evil - just look at Adolf Hitler! But - love trumps intelligence. It's better to have love in your heart than all the world's intelligence in your mind. Most of the things we do are temporary. Only our love and compassion for others is immortal. Your friends may forget what car you drove. They may forget the words you spoke or what you did for a living, but they certainly won't forget the love you have shown. Our display of compassion may be the only evidence non-believers have of God.

THERE'S A GREAT HUNGER IN THE LAND!

These days, people are hungrier than ever before. Their hunger is not a physical hunger. Theirs is a spiritual hunger. They are starving for love.

Recently, I was driving on the highway and I unintentionally cut off an elderly woman. I was so mortified. It was a mistake and I felt really bad about it. The woman, however, persisted in riding close behind me and screaming out curse words to me. She gave me one hand gesture after another. I thought to myself, *Man, this woman is not simply upset about me cutting her off. She seems to be upset about bigger issues.* Then my heart went out to her. I wondered what her home life was like. Why was she so angry? Had one of her family members severely hurt her? How could I pray for her? Clearly, this woman had a hunger for love.

UNCONDITIONAL LOVE?

The greatest gift you can give someone is unconditional love. We can buy material possessions, but we can't buy love. Without love, life is meaningless. Love makes the mundane things in life colorful.

Years ago while I was in New Orleans, I met a very angry teenager. This young man, Mike, was angry at the world. He had rejected Christ and wanted nothing to do with the church. I remember talking to him on several occasions about Christ, but he resisted wholeheartedly. As I was passing the street where he slept one night, God told me to give him my favorite shirt. At first I resisted, but I eventually gave it to him. The minute I gave him my shirt, everything changed! Mike said to me, "A lot of people told me about God but you were the first person to demonstrate God to me." For me, that day was a turning point of how I did ministry. I realized that great preaching is actually living the message. Concerning God's love, Mother Teresa said, "You know my God. My God is called love." We should be a tangible expression of Christ's love to this lonely and dying world.

BE THE PERSON WHO CARES

I once heard a story of a high school girl who was on the verge of suicide. She constantly was picked on at school. Her parents had abandoned her and she hated being in the foster care system.

At night she would stay up gazing at the ceiling wondering if anyone loved her. She felt as though she was ugly and worthless. No one had told her about God's amazing love. She believed the lie that her existence was pointless.

Then one day she thought to herself, "Today, I am going to walk through the mall. If I go through the entire mall and no one acknowledges me or says, 'hello' to me, I'm going to take my life." So she went to the mall. As she walked through the entire mall, not one person said hello or acknowledged her. So she went outside the mall and took her life.

I sometimes wonder how many times I walk past hurting people too busy to show them God's love. Our goal should be to always be there for people in need. Let's make it our mission to love others because their life might depend on it!

TWO TEENAGE PROSTITUTES

I remember going to Havana, Cuba to be a part of some evangelistic outreaches with the team I was with. It was there that we met two teenage prostitutes. They were poor, broken, and disillusioned by life. We shared the Good News with them but they had questions. One of the girls said, "If you guys really care for us, why don't you help us find a home?" We were totally caught off guard. Our team pulled our monetary resources together and got both of these young ladies a place to live. We connected them to a loving church in Cuba and today, both of these young ladies are off the streets and are living for God. At first, these girls didn't care about how much we knew about

God, they wanted to know if God cared about them. Our passion for God should show this hurting world that He really loves and cares for them. Are you willing to show radical compassion?

Taking Action!

1. Visit someone in a hospital, convalescent home, or jail this week.
2. Find out their story and encourage them.

Change from the Inside Out

Be the change you want to see in the world.
- Mahatma Gandhi

For it is by grace you have been saved,
through faith—and this not from yourselves,
it is the gift of God—not by works,
so that no one can boast.
- Ephesians 2:8-9

BE CHANGED TO MAKE A CHANGE

Most of this book has been about changing the world around you. But how can you change the world if you haven't been changed? You have to be changed to make a change. In others words, you have to be different in order to make a difference. Once our lives have been transformed by God's power, then we can help transform the world around us.

A SEARCH FOR MEANING

I can remember a time in my life when I was searching for meaning and purpose. I didn't have either one. My life was miserable each day as I searched without finding any answers. Maybe you are like I was, searching for hope. When we are sincere in our pursuit of Christ, He will reveal Himself to us! Are you ready to find out? If yes, then buckle your seat belts!

IT ALL STARTS WITH FAITH

A great definition for faith is "trusting God." Do you trust God completely? Most people struggle with this, but it is the only certain path to God. A great definition for doubt is not fully trusting in God.

Once there was a man who took a long hike up a mountain. After he was thousands of feet from the ground, he slipped and fell down the mountain. On his way down he grabbed hold of a branch. He looked down and saw he was hundreds of feet from the ground. He was sure he had come to his end. Then he called out to Jesus

Christ to save him. Jesus appeared with a host of angels singing praises.

The man said, "Jesus, if you save me I promise that I will turn my life around. I will stop cursing, using drugs, and partying! I promise!" Then Jesus asked the man if he was ready to trust him with everything. The man exclaimed, "Yes, Lord!" Then Jesus asked the man to let go of the branch and trust that He would catch him. At that, the man shouted for some other gods, "Mohammed! Buddha!" This man didn't fully trust Christ. However, the Bible tells us we must trust God with everything. When we let go of our lives, God comes in and changes us!

GOD KNEW WHAT WE NEEDED

God knew what man needed. If we needed a scientist to unlock the mysteries of God, He would have sent us a scientist. If we needed a political leader to help us, God would have sent a politician. If we needed a lot of money to go to heaven, He would have sent a banker. But we didn't need those things. We needed a Savior, so He sent Jesus Christ!

FOLLOWING CHRIST IS A BIG COMMITMENT

People will witness a noticeable change in us when we become Christians. In fact, the Apostle Paul says, *"Therefore, if anyone is in Christ, he is a new creation; the old has gone, the new has come!"* (2 Corinthians 5:17). When we come to God, our lives will change.

Recently, I was invited to share the gospel to a local

public school. One young girl responded to the message and was never the same. Her past was filled with promiscuity, drug use, and rebellion. One day one of her friends asked her to skip school so that they could go and use some drugs. She said, "I would go with you but I have changed. That was the old me!" Obviously, God had changed the life of this young lady. She understood that saying 'yes' to Jesus Christ means saying 'no' to all other vices and sin.

STEPS TO HAVING PEACE WITH GOD

First of all, you must admit your sins to God. The Bible says, "For all have sinned and fall short of the glory of God" (Romans 3:23). We have all blown it! God wants us to admit wrongs. Today, acknowledge that you are wrong.

Secondly, put your faith in the Cross of Christ. The cross represents God's payment for our sins. The Bible says, *"The wages for sin is death..."* (Romans 6:23). Jesus paid for our wrongdoings on the cross. In other words, God allowed man to beat on His Son so that He wouldn't have to beat on us! Jesus died in our place - what a wonderful Savior!

Thirdly, we must commit our entire lives to Jesus Christ. This type of commitment is exclusive. The Bible says, *"That if you confess with your mouth, "Jesus is Lord," and believe in your heart that God raised him from the dead, you will be saved"* (Romans 10:9). God want us to commit our lives to Him. Many people try to have Jesus along with some other idol in their lives. However, we can only serve one master.

Once while in India, a man who claimed to be Christian had a symbol of another god in his vehicle. Once I saw this I was blown away! I asked him if his wife would be okay with a picture of an ex-girlfriend in his car. He said, "No!" Then I said to him, "Why would God be okay with you trying to serve two masters?" Likewise, we can't serve the world and Christ at the same time. When we come to salvation in Christ, we turn everything over to Him! Are you ready to make Jesus the Boss of your life? Are you ready to ask for forgiveness for your sins? If the answer is yes, then wholeheartedly pray this prayer:

Dear Lord Jesus,

I invite You to come into my heart. I confess all my wrongdoings to You. Lord, heal me, deliver me, and set me free. I'm asking You to forgive me and make me a brand new person. I invite You to be my God, my Savior and best friend. I put my faith in all that Jesus did on the Cross. I no longer want to be the boss of my life. I give You my entire life. I am yours Lord, Forever. AMEN

SHARE IT WITH ME

If you prayed to receive Christ, please utilize my contact information on the back of this book to contact me. If you have been inspired to share your faith as a result of this book, please let me know as well. I am so ecstatic about what God is going to do through you!

WHY I BELIEVE IN THE GOOD NEWS?

First, I have personally seen my own life changed. Before I met Christ I was miserable. I was always searching for the next party and the next thrill. Today, I am content. I have inner peace. The anger and hostility I had in my heart have been replaced with love and joy. None of this would have been possible without Jesus Christ. Recently, I met up with an old friend I used to party with. He said, "Gibson, you have changed so much. It's like you're a totally different person." My friend is absolutely right. When I came to Christ, the old me died, and today, the new me is alive because of Jesus Christ!

Secondly, I believe in the Good News because I have seen it transform lives all over the world. The gospel has relevancy in every culture know to man. When I was in the Dominican Republic, I met a young man named Alex. Alex was known for his partying, womanizing, and drug abuse. He was the life of the party. A friend introduced me to Alex and we became friends instantly. I needed a translator, so I asked Alex to help me. He felt so happy that God could use his Spanish to make a difference. After spending a significant amount of time together, Alex confessed how miserable he was. He admitted that he was in need of some help to fight his addictions. We prayed, and Alex accepted Christ as his Savior. He gave up his worldly lifestyle and began serving God. Alex tried to give up drugs on his own, but only Jesus Christ could set him free. The Bible says, *"So if the Son sets you free, you will be free indeed"* (John 8:36). Jesus is in the business of transforming lives. When we put our trust in Him He will radically transform our lives!

Taking Action!

1. Find a new believer this week and encourage them in Christ.
2. Invite a non-believer to church this week.
3. Pray for opportunities to share the gospel this week.
4. If you prayed to receive Christ, please find a Bible-believing church and get connected.

Be Revolutionary!

A revival is nothing else than a new beginning of obedience to God.

- Charles Finney

*The world has yet to see
what God can do
with a man or woman
completely sold out to Christ.*

A SUDDEN CHANGE

A revolution is a sudden and radical change of order, socially, politically, intellectually, or religiously. When a revolution breaks out, major aspects of society change rapidly. We all love the story of Cinderella. She starts off being mistreated and despised by her stepmother and sisters, but when she meets the Prince, her life drastically changes. She goes from being a lowly servant to being royalty. The same is true for us. When we meet the Prince of Peace, Jesus Christ, a drastic change takes place in our lives.

This world has seen many types of revolutions, some for the good and some for the bad. The revolution I'm referring to is a revolution of love. We need revolution where we radically love God and love others. We need a revolution of being sacrificial instead of being selfish. We are in desperate need of a revolution of love! Are you ready for a revolution?

BURN THE SHIPS

I once heard a story about a general who had secretly landed on an island to capture it as his possession. During the night, he overheard some of his men planning to abandon their crew and sail back home to their families. The general became so angry that he ordered all of the ships to be burned at the dock. He told his troops, "Men, there is no turning back! Either you fight or die." What if we adopted that same mentality? Have you burned the ships to your past? The best way to move forward as a revolutionary for God is to burn your ships. Your ship can be a past sin. Completely eradicate that sin from your life. Perhaps it's a group of friends who have dragged you away from God in the past. Cut off all contact with them. Whatever vice we give up for Christ, He will bless us tenfold. Missionary Jim Elliot once said, "A man is not a fool who gives what he could never keep to gain what he can never lose." We must give our sins over to God for His blessings. Whenever we hold onto ungodly things, God isn't able to bless us with good things. A baby is born with a clinched fist; a man dies with an opened hand. We start our spiritual journeys holding onto our sin, then Christ calls us to die to ourselves. When our hands are opened, God can put anything He wants us to have in them. Burn the ships to your past and watch God open the floodgates of blessing in your life! Burn the ships to your past and get ready for a revolution!

SOUL ON FIRE!

In life, nothing of great significance can ever be accomplished without passion. In order to be revolutionary, you must have passion. Noah had great passion to obey God's Word, so he built the Ark. Michelangelo had a great passion for art, so he painted the roof of the Sistine Chapel in Rome. Martin Luther King, Jr. had a passion for equal rights, so he led the Civil Rights Movement. And last but not least, Gibson Sylvestre had a passion for Brigitte, so he married her! The point is that God gives us passion to accomplish the plans He calls us to. French soldier and theorist, Ferdinand Foch, put it this way, "The most

powerful weapon on earth is the human soul on fire."
What are you passionate about? What makes you
daydream during the day? Whenever someone mentions
my wife, they can physically observe my eyes light up.
When someone mentions how they are evangelizing a lost
neighbor, they can physically observe my eyes light up.
Why does my body react in this fashion? Because God has
given me a tremendous passion for these blessings. We will
look at some great ways we can direct our passion for God.

HAVE A PASSION FOR THE LORD!

When people look at your walk with God, they should
observe a passionate love affair. But it is so easy for our
relationship with Christ to grow cold and stale. Jesus
rebuked the believers in Revelation Chapter 2 because they
let their love grow cold. Is your fire flickering today? Then
all you have to do is ask Him and He'll fire you up again!
Oswald Chambers put it this way, "When we say, 'Speak,
Lord,' the romance begins." Make your relationship with
God romantic again. You can start by a simple whisper in
the ear of your Heavenly Father...

A PASSION FOR YOUR UNSAVED
FAMILY MEMBERS AND FRIENDS!

As others see your passion for Jesus Christ, they will
naturally be intrigued by it. Everyone likes a good love
story. John Wesley once said "If you set yourself on fire,
people will come from miles around to watch you burn!"
People who didn't even like the Apostle Paul were

impressed by his passion. Your passion for God will attract others to God. As you grow in passion for lost souls, God will bless you with opportunities to share your faith.

HAVE A PASSION FOR YOUR WORK!

Whenever we do our work with passion, the end result is obvious. If you don't have a passion for your job, then ask God for His grace. In Ecclesiastes King Solomon declared, *"Whatever your hand finds to do, do it with all your might..."* (Ecclesiastes 9:10) Whatever you do, whether it's school or work, pour yourself into it entirely. The Lord will be glorified through your work. Someone once said, "Life is not measured by the number of breaths we take but by the moments that take our breath away." As we live more passionately, we will see God do wonders.

STAY FIRED UP

We must commit to totally being sold out for Christ. Whenever I get discouraged God brings the poem "Fellowship of the Unashamed." Legend has it that it is the last words of a pastor who was martyred for Christ. Here are was his last words:

FELLOWSHIP OF THE UNASHAMED
(A Martyr's Last Words)

I am a part of the "Fellowship of the Unashamed." The die has been cast. I have stepped over the line. The decision has been made. I am a disciple of Jesus Christ. I won't look back, let up, slow down, back away, or be still.

My past is redeemed, my present makes sense, and my future is secure. I'm finished and done with low living, sight walking, small planning, smooth knees, colorless dreams, tame visions, mundane talking, cheap giving, and dwarfed goals.

My pace is set, my gait is fast, my goal is heaven, my road is narrow, my way is rough, my companions few, my guide reliable, my mission clear.

I won't give up, back up, let up or shut up until I've preached up, prayed up and paid up, stored up, and stayed up for the cause of Christ. I must go until He returns, give until I drop, preach until all I know, and work until He comes.

And when He comes to get His own, He will have no problem recognizing me. For my banner will be clear.

THE WORLD IS RADICAL

The world looks on at Christians and calls us radicals and fanatics. Consider this for a second. When it comes to football, Americans go ballistic. A typical football fan paints his face with his favorite team's logo. Then he spends a fortune on a team jersey and game ticket. Next he gets to the game three to four hours early. Then he drinks a lot of beer and vomits through most of the game. Half of the time he doesn't know what's going on. He does all of this, yet makes fun of his Christian co-worker for going to church on Sundays. It seems that in the world's eyes it's okay to be a fanatic for the things of the world as long as you're not a fanatic for God. Nothing can be more absurd! We must be proud of our relationship with God.

We can't be ashamed of it because it is the power of God. If is far better to please God than to please man. When you decide to be revolutionary for God, you will be persecuted. But stay with Jesus!

I heard a story of a pastor in China who was persecuted for his faith in Christ. One Sunday, as he was conducting one of his underground church services, a soldier burst through the door to arrest the congregation. The soldier said, "Everyone has thirty seconds to leave the church. Anyone who remains will be arrested and executed!" It a matter of seconds ninety-eight percent of the congregation had fled for their lives. The pastor, his wife, and daughter remained. They were singing songs to God because they knew they were going to die. The soldier asked the pastor, "Are you sure you don't want to leave and save your life?" The pastor answered, "I can not deny my Lord. I would rather die." Immediately, the soldier replied, "Pastor, I am Christian as well. I was just seeing who the real Christians were. You may continue with the service." Our goal should be to have the same boldness and radical love of that Chinese pastor who was willing to die for Christ!

REVOLUTIONARY PROMISES

In these last days, God is looking for men and women with revolutionary faith. For years, I lived with a fear of expressing my faith. God convicted me and exhorted me to live for Him boldly. I used to be bold for the things of the world. Sin gripped my heart. Now I have the joy of expressing my boldness for God. I now live by the revolutionary pledge. Carefully read it. Carefully consider the commitment. Then after you've prayed and feel that it's right, sign it and commit to live by it for the rest of your life.

REVOLUTIONARY PLEDGE

I commit my life, my dreams, and purpose to the cause of Christ. I will not give up, let up, let in, or slow down. My life is His.

I refuse to go with the flow. I refuse to barely get by. I will make a difference in someone else's life.

I refuse to allow my identity to be confined to the things of this world. For I am only a stranger in a far away land. My only home is Heaven.

I endeavor to walk by faith and not by fear, to walk by faith and not by sight, for I am committed to walk in faith and not by my feelings! I've made up my mind to walk in God's ways, even when it hurts.

I commit to being others-centered rather than self-centered. I choose to be last instead of first. I choose to give before I take and listen before I demand.

For me, success will not be measured by how many times I fall, but by how many times I get back up. I realize that before I can change the world, I must allow God to first change me. I realize that in order to make a difference, I must first be different.

I commit to submitting to the leadership of the Holy Spirit with all of my heart to the best of my ability. I realize that my participation as a member of the Body of Christ is a privilege and call from God, not a right. I further commit to the cause of spreading the gospel. I positively do this with all my heart, my mind, my body, my soul and my all.

I give all that I am and all that I am not to the "Jesus Revolution." I understand that it may not be easy, but I was not called to that which is easy. I am called to change the world!

Even if 40% of the world doesn't stand for Jesus' Revolution, I will stand.
Even if 70 % of this world doesn't stand for Jesus' Revolution, I will stand.

I will stand for Christ even if 99% of the world turns their back on His Revolution.
Even If I found out tomorrow that I was the only one in the entire world who still believed,
I would stand.
Because I am a REVOLUTIONARY!

(Sign here if you believe this wholeheartedly!)   *(Date)*

GOD ALWAYS PRESERVES A
REMNANT FOR HIS REVOLUTION

The word "remnant" implies someone who is a survivor or someone who remains standing when all others have fallen. This is exactly what a revolutionary is. The Bible says *"Unless the Lord Almighty had left us some survivors, we would have become like Sodom, we would have been like Gomorrah"* (Isaiah 1:9). God will always provide a group of people set apart for His purposes. When the world tells us "no," God reverses the letters and turns it to "on." God wants to do a special work in our midst. Mildred Cable put it this way, "God provides the men and women needed for each generation." God wants to use you. Are you willing to be set apart for the Lord?

CROSSING THE RUBICON

Are ready to cross the Rubicon? The Rubicon is the point of no return. This is the where you leave a life of mediocrity for a live of reckless abandonment for Christ. Years ago I was in a season where I was struggling with my commitment to Christ. I sat down at wrote this poem I'm about to share with you. This poem has helped me tremendously. When I start to get cold or lukewarm I read it and it fires me up again. Here it is:

THE REMNANT

There is a cry from the lowest pit of God's people. A people on whom curses have been spoken. Where the cord of a bright future has been said to have been broken. A people plagued with recklessness, despair and hopelessness. A people in the twilight of histories darkest light. Battered, broken, blinded and burdened. A confused people like flies running wildly in their minds with tragic travesties displayed at Columbine. A people in desperate need of a cure, trapped in darkness, barricaded, searching to find an open door. Despite all the oppositions who oppose this people there shall be a regeneration.

Almighty God has orchestrated and ordained a remnant. A remnant appointed and anointed vigilantes tired of seeing God's people robbed and conformed to society's moral filth. A remnant of diligent, vigilant, vigilante soldiers of righteousness. They refuse to allow their voices to be silenced by today's popular opinions in today's society. They refuse to allow today's music to shape their thoughts. They refuse to go with the flow. They refuse to do enough just to get by. They refuse to allow their identities to be defined by the clothes they wear. They have one-track minds and will not stop until they witness an insurmountable shift and turn of God's people. They are not ashamed to be rejected and to be the minority. They will not stop or conform to the patterns of this world. They are destined, determined, not demanding, but certainly outstanding. They are the initiators not imitators. They are today's learners and tomorrow's leaders. They don't merely talk it but walk it. They are committed to building godly relationships, strong families, and to restoring the brokenhearted. They forget the past, live in the present, and allow God to deal with the future. They abolish excuses and only get stronger in *adversity. They defeat the two evils; procrastination and hesitation. They seize today knowing that tomorrow may never come! They are compelled by a sense of urgency that they must reclaim their nation for Christ. Setbacks won't set them back! They are desperately dependent upon a great awakening outpouring of the Holy Spirit. They are God's warriors. God's remedy is this remnant! God's preserved and reserved. They live by and hold themselves to the highest moral standards. They will be the catalyst of the next riveting, roaring, and rejuvenating revival! Get ready America, here we come!*

WILL YOU PRAY FOR REVIVAL?

What will history say about us? Will you be a world-changer for Christ? The world has yet to see what God can do with a man or woman completely sold out to God. Why can't you be the one? Who says God can't use you to change the world. I met a gentleman who said to me, "Why do you believe God can use someone to change the world? Isn't that being unrealistic?" Yes, I know the odds are against anyone who thinks they can change the world. I would rather attempt mighty things and fail, than to just sit back and do nothing. Former United States President, Theodore Roosevelt, put it this way, "Far better is it to dare mighty things, to win glorious triumphs, even though checked by failure...than to rank with those poor spirits who neither enjoy much nor suffer much, because they live in a gray twilight that knows not victory nor defeat." Will you be someone who "dares mighty things" for God? The good news is God never intended for us to do those mighty things alone. God is changing the world through His body, the Church!

Can you imagine a great awakening sweeping your city, your state, and your country? Historically, when God brings revival businesses close early because people are busy attending church services. Major sports events are canceled because the people and the players would rather go to church and praise God. Huge numbers of people come to Christ. Crime rates drop. Divorce rates drop. Families are restored. God's people get busy caring for the poor, abused, and neglected in their communities. Prisons are empty. Churches unite and share resources. Wow, wouldn't this be remarkable? The scriptures declare, *"If my people, who are called by my name, will humble themselves and pray and seek my face and turn from their wicked ways, then will I hear from heaven and will forgive their sin and will heal their land"* (II Chronicle 7:14). It all begins with prayer. Our hearts unite with God's heart in prayer. Will you pray for revival? Furthermore, we must seek God's face. Seeking has to do with desperation. As I said earlier, the degree of our desperation will be the degree of God's saturation. Will you seek God's face? Then we must repent or turn from our sinful ways. Let's live lives of holiness. When we live clean lives, God's blessing rests upon us. Will you commit to walking in holiness? When we will get right with God, He promises to heal our land. When revival comes, the lost are saved! When revival comes, the prodigal son comes home. When revival comes, cities are transformed by the power of God! All the men and women God has used were ordinary people who were courageous because they knew that God was with them. This world is desperately crying out for men and women with an authentic passion for God. Will you be one of them?

Taking Action!

1. What action steps can you take to increase your passion for the Lord?
2. What is something you can do to further cement your decision to follow God?